MW01223177

Joachim Grupp

SHOTOKAN KARATE

Kihon, Kumite, Kata

Meyer & Meyer Sport

Original title: Shotokan Karate: Training und Technik;
mit aktueller Prüfungsordnung/Joachim Grupp.
- Aachen: Meyer & Meyer Verlag, 2001
Translated by James Beachus

British Library Cataloguing in Publication Data
A catalogue record for this book is available from the British Library

Grupp, Joachim:
Shotokan Karate - Kihon, Kumite, Kata
Oxford: Meyer & Meyer Sport (UK) Ltd., 2002
ISBN 1-84126-071-1

All rights reserved, especially the right to copy and distribute, including the translation rights. No part of
this work may be reproduced – including by photocopy, microfilm or any other means – processed, stored
electronically, copied or distributed in any form whatsoever without the written permission of the publisher.

© 2002 by Meyer & Meyer Sport (UK) Ltd.
Aachen, Adelaide, Auckland, Budapest, Graz, Johannesburg,
Miami, Olten (CH), Oxford, Singapore, Toronto
Member of the World
Sports Publishers' Association (WSPA)
www.w-s-p-a.org

Printed and bound in Germany
by: Druckpunkt Offset GmbH, Bergheim
ISBN 1-84126-071-1
E-Mail: verlag@meyer-meyer-sports.com
www.meyer-meyer-sports.com

SHOTOKAN KARATE

Contents

SHOTOKAN KARATE

Kihon, Kumite, Kata

In the 1950s, Japanese Karate was introduced into the Western world. Today Karate is an established sport, and after Judo it is the most popular of the martial arts. In Japanese Karate-Do there are several styles, which despite having similarities with each other, can be individually distinguished from one another, with each style having its own techniques and katas. The most popular style worldwide as well as in Germany is Shotokan Karate. Alone in my home country, Germany, there are about 140,000 people practising Karate, of which over 90% are following the Shotokan style.

The historical section in this book traces the history of Karate up to today's Shotokan Karate as well as the principles of "Do" in Karate. This could not be possible without paying tribute to the life work of both of the fathers of Shotokan Karate - Gichin Funakoshi and Masatoshi Nakayama.

Karate is divided into three areas; Kihon (Basic techniques), Kumite (exercises with a partner) and Kata (forms). "Shotokan Karate, Kihon, Kumite, Kata" comprehensively covers many of the important basic techniques. It includes numerous suggestions for training in the Kihon techniques and the classic Kumite forms. Gohon Kumite, Kihon-Ippon Kumite, Kaeshi-Ippon Kumite, Jiyu-Ippon Kumite and Jiyu-Kumite are all covered in depth. The basic Katas, Heian 1-5, Tekki 1 and Bassai-Dai are dealt with in the section on Katas.

With the inclusion of exact illustrations and descriptions, this compact aid strives to assist all Shotokan Karatekas in improving their technical abilities in a fun and energetic way.

Joachim Grupp

1.1 History of Shotokan Karate
1.1.1 Okinawa-Te - the Origin of Modern Karate

Karate-Do, as we know it today, is a type of martial art steeped in tradition, but nonetheless relatively new. A glance at its history shows how this apparent contradiction can be explained.

Okinawa, which is the country of origin for Karate, is the largest of the Ryukyu group of islands and lies about 500 kilometres from the Japanese island Kyushu and about 800 kilometres off Foochow on the Chinese mainland.

The island, whose inhabitants lived mainly from fishing and agriculture as well as trade with neighbouring countries, was divided into three kingdoms up until the 15th Century. These provinces - Chuzan, Nanzan and Hokuzan - waged violent war amongst themselves. Even before the unification of the three regions in 1429 under the King of Chuzan, Sho Hashi, the island occupied an important position as the centre of the flourishing trade with the neighbouring countries of China, Korea, Taiwan and Japan, due to its geographical location. The influx of cultural and political influences associated with the import trade contributed also to the spread of regional martial arts from other Asiatic countries into certain regions of Okinawa.

While this influence centred itself round the commercial centres of Shuri, Naha and Tomari, it nevertheless helped the widely different martial arts gain enormous popularity. Worthy of mention in this connection is the knowledge of handling weapons, which came with Japanese refugees to Okinawa as early as the 10th Century. There is the bow and arrow, or use of the sword (Katana and Tachi) as well as the numerous hard and soft styles of the Chinese art of Chuan-Fa, held as the forerunner of today's Kung-Fu.

Even if in several versions of the history of Karate it is erroneously maintained that the Chinese taught martial arts to the inhabitants of Okinawa, and that they then developed the system of Karate from this, those better informed insist that the older martial art of Te (Te=hand) existed on Okinawa already and was taught there by several masters. It is less probable that the Chinese - who considered themselves socially and culturally superior - systematically gave instruction in these arts. It is more likely that the Chinese influence worked more indirectly. Thus the various

The History

OKINAWA-TE

Okinawan envoys from the regent King Satto in 1372 brought back elements of Chinese martial arts to the island. Here the martial arts were always only carried out by a few in small schools and passed on in the family circle or amongst friends. This also would explain the different versions, which can be found in the native Te. It cannot be said that Te became something like a popular sport. It was the martial art carried out by only a few select insiders.

A direct Chinese influence came when a group of 36 Chinese families settled in the vicinity of Naha called Kumemura in 1392. From here they introduced the local inhabitants to Zen-Buddhism, teaching them their religion and philosophy. It is possible that they had an influence on the development of Te in the Naha region. It is held that the local popular Naha-Te (later called Shorei-Ryu – 'Ryu' means 'school' or 'way of') was inspired from the traditions of Chuan-Fa. It consists of dynamic movements and lays value on breathing and the technique of the production of rapid and explosive power. Other centres for Te were Tomari and Shuri (the styles developed here were later also called Shorin-Ryu). A Chinese influence could also be found in Shuri-Te with its emphasis on breathing control and round defensive movements. Tomari-Te contains both these elements and concentrates on flexible rapid movements.

The American author Randall HASSELL, who has written one of the best well-researched books about the history of Shotokan, separates the local native techniques of Te into two differing martial art systems. The one style, preferred by the rural inhabitants, uses a low stance so that defence is executed from low down with the arms and legs, while the other more powerful style uses numerous strong arm movements and can be traced back to the fishermen.

Besides this, the inhabitants of Okinawa were very creative in the use of their tools as weapons against the marauding Samurai and against plundering invaders and pirates. The use of these tools as defensive instruments was called Kobudo and they consisted of items such as Bo, Tonfa, Nunchaku, Eku, Kama, Kusarigama and other equipment. Dependent on the type of "weapon" these permitted close quarter and distant fighting. Many Kata techniques still contain defensive movements against attacks carried out using these "tools". When, for the first time under the reign of Sho Shin (1477-1526), the use of weapons was banned, these tools were replaced with unobtrusive harmless everyday fisherman's and farming implements, and these skills became popular as well as unarmed defensive combat.

OKINAWA-TE

The strong Japanese influence since the occupation of the island by the Ieshisa Shimazu clan in 1609 (also called the period of control by the Satsuma dynasty) brought considerable suppression of the people; even the use of ceremonial swords and arming of servants of the state was forbidden. The population stood literally "empty handed".

Changing occupying forces, suppression by new rulers and the necessity to defend oneself against often life threatening attacks made Te and Kobudo more popular. This always occurred in small circles, which developed their own system in such a way that were enough to meet their particular defensive requirements. The efficiency of unarmed-combat led to the Japanese also banning it.

The masters of the various systems could therefore only pass on their knowledge in secret, which again prevented the development of a standardised "Okinawa style". The population held these masters in great respect. Some masters passed on the techniques in the form of encoded movement sequences called Kata. Today's common interpretation of the term Kata as 'form, sequence' is inadequate. The fact that constant practice of the movements until perfection was reached served to improve the technique and control of the body, it was the dividing line in earnest against an armed aggressor and was the difference between life or death. In order to improve their techniques, the Okinawans used several aids. The best known of these was the Makiwara – a punch bag fixed to a post. To master Te it was necessary to be able to distinguish amongst the possible techniques, and be able to concentrate totally on the selected one, so that the aggressor was put out of action with the first blow. It was often the case that the aggressor were heavily armed Samurai, who tried to fill their own war coffers at the expense of the people.

The end of the Satsuma regime in 1872 and the Meiji government reforms in Japan in 1868 created a liberalisation of the whole Japanese society and all of the principles of the feudalistic class society were brought down. Modern transport means, emerging world-wide trade, and with it, contact with other continents and cultures created an opening of the Japanese society and its values to the rest of the world.

As Okinawa officially was part of Japan since 1875, the island also profited from this opening. Naturally this also included Okinawa-Te or Tang-Te, as the unarmed art on Okinawa was called after the Tang dynasty (Tang=Chinese). From this time Te could be freely followed officially. In order to understand modern Karate properly

The History

OKINAWA-TE

it is necessary to remember the fact that the Japanese, while exercising control over the island as part of Japan, always distrusted the Okinawan culture, did not recognise it or scorned it as backward.

At the end of the 19th Century one could not speak of a standardised style of martial art in Okinawa. As already mentioned, in the course of the century a large number of schools and styles had been developed, of which Naha-Te, Shuri-Te and Tomari-Te were the most well-known. It is difficult in today's terms to call the Te forms different styles, since the repertoire of some masters consisted of either only a single or very few techniques. It is reported of one master, that he spent his whole life practising a blow using the elbow. Sometimes the farmers or fishermen, who used these blows or kicks, were well-known for one single technique. They had practised it for the whole of their lives and perfected it with great efficiency. On the other hand there were masters who had begun to develop complete systems.

The historian REILLY tells us that there was great rivalry between the large schools of Shuri-Te, Naha-Te and Tomari-Te following official recognition of their arts. Quarrels between the various schools added to damaging the esteem of Te on Okinawa. Despite this, the popularity of (Kara-) Te grew. Shintaro Ogawa, the official responsible for school education in the prefecture of Kagoshima, appointed the Master Anko Itosu to be Instructor of Training in the elementary schools. He had been impressed by the demonstration performed by a young man, whose group of pupils showed extraordinarily good body condition – his name was Gichin FUNAKOSHI. In 1902, (Kara-) Te became a school sport on Okinawa.

MODERN KARATE

1.1.2 Modern Karate Comes into Being

Where the original aim of Te served to be the physical destruction of the opponent, often armed, its development as a school sport marked a turn. Not only did it mean that there was a change from being something secretive, only available to a selected few, to being an official part of the school curriculum, it also heralded the change from being a deadly fighting method to being a type of sport that serves to further the character and train the body.

This new aspect of Karate, where now the training was based on the improvement of the condition and outlook of the pupils, has its roots in the time of Okinawa-Te at the turn of the century. Likewise, the term "Kara-Te" was first used around this time. "Tang" means China and "Kara" is the Japanese translation of the word. The term "Chinese hand" expresses the respect that Okinawa had for China. In 1904 the way of writing Karate was changed for the first time in a book written about Karate. The author was Chomo HANAGI and he reflected in his writing the increasing leaning towards Japanese nationalism and the growing rejection of any Chinese influence in Okinawa and Japan.

In 1922, FUNAKOSHI changed the name for all time by writing the Japanese character symbol for "Kara" (meaning 'empty') instead of the symbol "Kara" meaning 'Chinese'. Thus the meaning of "Karate" was thereafter known as 'empty hand' meaning the common name for the systematic method of Karate.

1.1.3 Gichin Funakoshi – the Father of Modern Karate

Without the actions of Gichin FUNAKOSHI, the large popularity of Karate in Japan would not be possible. The son of a civil servant, he was born in Shuri in 1868. Early on he was able to learn the Chinese language, and at the age of eleven years old he came into contact with Karate through a school friend. His friend's father was Yatsutsune AZATO, one of the most respected masters of Shuri-Te. FUNAKOSHI, generally regarded as the founder of modern Karate and in particular the Shotokan style, developed into being one of the best students of the master AZATO, and he later came under the master ITOSU. He became a teacher and besides his extraordinary capability of perfecting the techniques of Te, also had an excellent artistic and linguistic talent.

GICHIN FUNAKOSHI

Gichin Funakoshi

Contrary to other masters, who wanted to continue to practice Karate partially in a secretive manner, he had the drive of a missionary wanting to perform his art widely to the public striving to systemise and build-up Karate anew. His performances, which he carried out together with other Okinawan Karate experts (amongst whom was the founder of the Shito-Ryu style – Kenwa MABUNI), were so popular, that the Ministry of Education asked FUNAKOSHI, in 1917, to give a demonstration with his assistants at Kyoto in Japan. This was the first time that Karate had been demonstrated outside Okinawa.

In 1921, when the Japanese Crown Prince, visiting Okinawa, saw one of FUNAKOSHI's performances, he was so impressed that he invited him to give further demonstrations in Japan. FUNAKOSHI, who was asked by the Ministry of Education to agree to the Crown Prince's request, was at that time chairman of the Okinawan Shobukai, an association set up to spread the word on the Okinawan martial arts. In this function he put his keen sense for effective public relations work to the test for the first time. He followed up the request and went to Japan. The triumph march of Karate as a martial art had begun.

FUNAKOSHI, who had gradually continued to integrate philosophical principles into his system and used Karate as a school for the improvement of the character, saw it as the unity of both the body and the mind. He had already changed the symbol for Karate into something which matched his philosophical convictions as well as coming closer to the Zen philosophy. The term "empty hand" was at the root of the Zen principle of "letting go of earthly things". The spirit was to be freed of those worldly thoughts, which would prevent the development of the unity of body and mind.

FUNAKOSHI combined the basics of Zen, which were close to his thinking, with the art of fighting. The change in the name and the methodical structure of Karate expressed in his book "Ryukyu Kempo: Karate" in 1922 made him even more famous. This book was illustrated by the famous artist Hoan KOSUGI, who later designed the symbol for Shotokan (Tiger in the circle). It contained a method

GICHIN FUNAKOSHI

already, which was to be the pointer to the future for later text books by the JKA (Japan Karate Association).

He won the hearts and minds of the Japanese upper-class with his performances in the "Dai Nippon Butotukai" when he demonstrated his own martial art style alongside the well established martial arts of Kendo and Judo in Japan. Having seen his demonstration, numerous influential Japanese persuaded him to stay in Japan. The few planned weeks, that he had originally wished to devote for his period of instruction in Japan, turned into a long phase in his life until his death in 1957. Karate, the martial art of the Okinawan farmers and fishermen

Shotokan Emblem/
Tiger in the circle

had quickly become a Japanese Budo discipline. It was now followed and practised mainly by the upper-class and intellectuals at universities and in the military.

As a result of the 'Japanisation' of Karate, further famous ' founders of the style', such as MABUNI (Shito-Ryu) and MIYAGI (Goju-Ryu) came to Japan later, and gave instruction in their interpretation of Karate.

FUNAKOSHI 's popularity knew no bounds. As a well educated master, he could speak and write fluent Japanese, which was something the other Okinawan Karate instructors could not do. Also as a calligrapher of his own poetry, which he published under his artist's name "SHOTO", his popularity rose even more because of this. Further demonstrations followed, including performing in front of family members of the King in the Japanese Palace. Instructing in schools and universities every day, FUNAKOSHI became the vogue for the new Japanese Budo discipline of Karate. The master of this new "Japanese" martial art was so popular that he gave instruction to masters of other Budo disciplines. For example he gave instruction to the founder of modern Iaido and to Jigorono KANO, the founder of Judo. He showed the latter the Kata Kanku Dai and Tekki in the stronghold of Judo - Kodokan.

The first of the universities where he gave instruction was the Keio University and shortly afterwards others followed in taking up his methods - Tokyo, Hosei, Nihon and Shodai -the most well known was later to become the Takushoku University

("Takudai"). The strong embodiment of his Karate methods in the universities laid the cornerstone for the world-wide popularity of Shotokan later.

However, in Okinawa, many of the old masters came out against the leaning towards systematic methods and the development of the Japanese discipline. They saw in FUNAKOSHI a traitor to the traditions of Okinawa-Te. This, however, did not halt the triumphant drive forward of modern Karate. A little later on many of his critics also took up the definition of Karate for their own martial art.

1.1.4   Shotokan Karate Spreads World-wide

Between 1930 and 1935, FUNAKOSHI developed the common Kumite forms used still today – Gohon Kumite, Kihon - Ippon Kumite, Jiyu - Ippon Kumite and Jiyu - Kumite. Using the partner oriented exercises, he had found an effective instrument, which would bring greater emphasis to the aspect of self-defence. Kata exercises served also to train for flexibility, speed and power. Gradually, one also took note of an aesthetic dimension in practice of Kata. Up until then, FUNAKOSHI's Karate training, and other styles carried out in schools, had consisted almost exclusively of repetitive Kata exercises and intensive Makiwara training.

In order to develop Kumite, individual passages were taken out of the Kata and practised as attack-defence situations. Despite the new division into three sections of Kihon, Kata and Kumite (Basic Technique, Partner exercises, Forms), according to Masatoshi NAKAYAMA, who trained under FUNAKOSHI from 1932, training was still the same as held in the philosophy of Ikken Hissatsu – the art of stopping or killing the opponent with one single blow. Each technique was exercised and repeated meticulously and repetitively up to total exhaustion. The concept of the Ippon comes from the traditional view of one single action when a fight can be ended. Today's training routine is mostly far removed from the unimaginable intensity and severity of training in those days.

The first independent Karate dojo, world-wide, was inaugurated by FUNAKOSHI on 29th January 1939. His influential students, coming from all over Japan, had raised the financial means to give the master, now at the ripe old age of 71, this honour. Over the entrance they had placed the inscription "Shotokan" (The Hall of Shoto) – a term used by his students from that day for the FUNAKOSHI style. Besides Gishin FUNAKOSHI, his son Yoshitaka "Giko" FUNAKOSHI (who died 1945) also taught in

SHOTOKAN KARATE

the master's private house, at universities and, later, in the central Dojo. Several changes in the Kata and basic start positions, as authorised by his father, can be attributed to him. For example he developed the Kata Sochin from the old, largely rudimentary, handed-down guidelines. Gradually, the varied core for a new, all-embracing fighting system was created. Gichin FUNAKOSHI brought to the fore yet a further, important step towards the 'Japanisation' of his style in his book "Karate-Do Kyohan", which was published in 1936. In this he changed the names of the Kata and gave them Japanese ones.

At that time, some of the 70 or more styles of Karate were established by students, who had very little knowledge of Karate since they had only been training for a few years. This brought with it increasing confusion for the general public. In order to build-up organisational structures and to give a visibility to the high training standards of his pupils, FUNAKOSHI and many of his followers – some of whom, in the meanwhile, had become instructors also – were faced with a new challenge. In 1936 the "All Japan Collegiate Union" was founded – one of the first collectives of the university Dojos mainly in the tradition of FUNAKOSHI.

Up until the foundation of the "Japan Karate Association" (JKA) in 1949, the Second World War and the American occupation of Japan brought a compulsory halt to the further development of Shotokan Karate as well as the other styles, which had evolved such as Goju-Ryu, Wado-Ryu and Shito-Ryu. At the end of the war the Americans had banned all Budo disciplines. The formation of the JKA in 1949 as an association embraced all those Dojos, university clubs and Karate groups, which practised FUNAKOSHI's style. FUNAKOSHI was named as the Chief Instructor. The other main styles of Goju-Ryu, Shito-Ryu and Wado-Ryu also formed their own organisations, which then in 1965 joined together along with the Shotokan Association, the JKA as the "big four" into the FAJKO (Federation of All Japan Karate-Do Organisation) without giving up their own independence.

After the war there were then several factors, which were decisive for the enormous popularity of Shotokan and its final development into a comprehensive martial art system. Worthy of mention is the large interest that the US servicemen showed for Karate in occupied Japan. This corresponded with FUNAKOSHI's mission to establish Karate world-wide. At the age of 83, together with his best students NAKAYAMA, OBATA and NISHIJAMA, he travelled round numerous air bases of the S.A.C. (Strategic Air Command) in order to give Karate performances with his team.

MASATOSHI NAKAYAMA

The popularity rose around the world and the soldiers returning home formed their own Dojos and later brought Japanese JKA instructors into the USA.

The requirement for trained instructors brought about the next development. Under FUNAKOSHI's eye, instructor courses lasting several years were set up in the Takushoku University for the best JKA Karateka. The instructor programme was set up by NAKAYAMA, OKAZAKI and NISHIJAMA. All three were leading representatives in the JKA. The development of one of the strictest and hardest training programmes provided the ability to send out over 30 of the best well-trained Karate instructors across the world between 1957 and 1970. These brilliant masters of the technique and fighters spread the word on Shotokan Karate internationally as we know it today. Masters of Karate such as KANAZAWA, ENOEDA, KASE, SHIRAI, NAITO, OKAZAKI, SUGIMURA and many others represent, still today, an unbeatable measure of quality and the high standard of Shotokan for most of the European, Asiatic and American Karate instructors.

1.1.5 The Development of Shotokan by Masatoshi Nakayama

While still under FUNAKOSHI, the basis for the high standard was created by the JKA using a scientific establishment of the Karate techniques and introducing competitions. The man, who FUNAKOSHI entrusted with this was none other than Masatoshi NAKAYAMA. After FUNAKOSHI's death in 1957 he inherited his role and was named as the main functionary of the JKA. After his studies, NAKAYAMA, who had lived a long time in China from where he had brought new techniques such as Ura-Mawashi-Geri, enjoyed FUNAKOSHI's complete confidence. He had always also studied the less-known styles in order to incorporate the essentials into his system e.g., the original Goju Kata Hangetsu. As early as the 1930's, NAKAYAMA had been tasked with learning and adapting the Kata Gojushiho and Nijushiho from the master MABUNI into the Shotokan style. Together with FUNAKOSHI he continued to develop the system into a comprehensive martial art, and this soon contained all the facets. The simple and rapid elements of Shorin-Ryu as well as the complex and breathing emphasised elements of the Shorei-Ryu are all amply contained in Shotokan.

MASATOSHI NAKAYAMA

The necessity of scientific embodiment as a basis for Shotokan Karate was recognised by FUNAKOSHI and NAKAYAMA in 1953 as they gave instruction to the first US soldiers. NAKAYAMA reported about the unusual questioning by the 'Gaijin' regarding the 'Why?", "How?" and "Wherefore?' which they made during training. In the Japanese routine of training this sort of questioning was unknown. Here it was merely a question of doggedly practising 'until perfect' that lay in the foreground and not one of 'Why?'. Instructor's publications, mainly the works of NAKAYAMA, which then appeared based on the FUNAKOSHI traditions, illustrated the basics of the styles all founded on the technique according to medical, anatomical, and physiological reasoning.

After long deliberations, in 1956, the JKA put together the first book of regulations and carried out the first All Japan Championships in 1957. The difficulty in working up the competition rules was in sorting out the numerous dangerous techniques, over which control was hardly if not impossible to maintain, as well as finalising and testing protective equipment and a point system. Protective equipment was abandoned because it restricted the freedom of movement. Parallel to the Kumite competitions, the JKA functionaries assembled together rules for the judging of comparisons of Kata disciplines. It can be noted that the idea of the competition system was to follow FUNAKOSHI's own interest in his tradition of retaining the broadest possible spectrum of public interest and making it available to the masses.

Even long before the JKA instructors gave thought to compiling a book of rules, which on the one hand was true to the basics of Karate, and on the other ensured the safety of the opponent as an overriding aim, there had been "comparison bouts" between some of the Te schools. NAKAYAMA reports in a series of biographical interviews (appearing also as a book) with the American author HASSELL that these bouts always ended up in bloody fights, and that several Karateka had emerged from these 'comparisons' with severe injuries. In post-war Japan, where the populace had seen enough of war and fighting, it was now important to do justice to the traditions and challenges so that maximum sport could be achieved from the result of producing a suitable and adaptable set of regulations. The sporting aspects and competitive factor became the last building block.

MASATOSHI NAKAYAMA

Masatoshi Nakayama

It is, however, important to remember that FUNAKOSHI, as well as his successor NAKAYAMA, always referred to the priority role of basic training and Kata, and warned against a form of Karate that only aimed at success in competitions. From today's point of view this can only be supported. The length of the ability of a Karateka being able to compete is about 10-15 years and is the shortest period in his life of the sport he has chosen for life. However, it is good experience for a small number of all Karateka – say 5-10% – as they come very close to a serious self-defense situation.

All this is a border-line experience, which can contribute to the improvement of the character and, of course, can add to the improvement of one's ability to be able to act coolly and more determinedly in a situation requiring self-defence. The legends carry on persistently still today: FUNAKOSHI had always disapproved of the idea of turning Karate into merely a sport, as well as the JKA as an organisation that encouraged sport as one part of Karate. As the reformer of modern Karate, he knew only too well that this aspect was necessary in order to make Karate an equal to the other Budo disciplines in Japan.

Whoever grumbles about the sporting aspects and makes a comparison with the supposedly "natural and original" aspects, overlooks the fact that only a minority practice Karate as a competitive sport. Moreover, he must ask himself how far back his reckoning of time goes. Where is this so-called 'natural and original' Karate traced back to? Should this go back to before 1902 when Karate was a school sport? Even Karate could not escape progress and FUNAKOSHI was the driving force behind this development. In reflecting all this, remember that he and his pupils created a system with which one should compare the philosophical and technical quality of today's Karate.

FUNAKOSHI was not able to experience, however, the last facet of his comprehensive martial art method. In the same year as the first competition Karate the master died. According to Teruyuki OKAZAKI, he had still given regular daily

SHOTOKAN KARATE TODAY

instruction in the central Dojo of the JKA right up to a few days prior to his death. The JKA – the only organisation that he had authorised – carried on FUNAKOSHI's mission to spread the word on Karate under the leadership of Masatoshi NAKAYAMA with great success.

1.1.6 Shotokan Karate Today

Up to the present day, the JKA theory of teaching the Shotokan style still remains the method used by the majority of the estimated four million Karateka world-wide. Despite this the JKA, as an organisation for the Shotokan Karateka, has lost a lot of the sparkle and meaning, which it enjoyed up to NAKAYAMA's death in 1987. Not least of all because of the formation of several splinter groups – to the organisational detriment of the JKA – such as the foundation of the association "Shotokan Karate International" (SKI) by the famous H. KANAZAWA in 1977. In addition to this, the JKA broke up into two fractions in 1990.

In spite of this, their technical guidelines remain as the benchmark for the Shotokan style. For example, in Germany the grading programme for Shotokan Karate used by the DKV (German Karate Association) is based exclusively on the high technical standard, which had been set by the life work of FUNAKOSHI for his charismatic pupils. Written in the charter are the words; "The execution of the techniques is to be according to the methods given in M. NAKAYAMA's book KARATE-DO". Thus the measure of quality is taken from those expressed by the most advanced Shotokan master up until today.

1.1.7 Karate in Germany – the Author's Home Country

The international spread of Karate, and in particular Shotokan, rapidly increased in pace after 1945 assisted considerably by FUNAKOSHI's pupils. While, already at the beginning of the '50's, the first instructors from Japan were working in the USA, the spread of Karate in Europe, using trained instructors, did not come in until the end of the '50's.

In Germany, it was introduced by Jürgen SEYDEL, who had watched performances of Karate in France. In 1961, several pioneers of Karate founded the Deutsche Karate Bund (German Karate Union) followed by other Associations, which all formed into

SHOTOKAN KARATE

the Deutsche Karate Verband e.V (DKV) (German Karate Association). Today the DKV represents the majority of the Shotokan Karateka as well as Karateka from other traditional styles in Germany. As the country's foremost Karate Association, it offers its members the whole spectrum of the sport, from recreational through to competitive support, having a good complement of well trained instructors and grading officials together in more than 2,000 clubs. The DKV is officially recognised by the Deutsche Sportbund (DSB) (German Sports Union) as the specialist sporting association for Karate in the country. As a member of the International Karate Organisation – the WKF (World Karate Federation), which is officially recognised by the IOC (International Olympic Committee) – it allows the DKV athletes a sporting opportunity at world level.

1.2   Karate Do

"JUST AS THE FLAT SURFACE OF THE MIRROR REFLECTS ALL THAT STANDS BEFORE IT, AND LIKE IN A QUIET VALLEY EVEN ECHOES THE MOST SILENT SOUND, THE KARATEKA SHOULD FREE HIS INNER THOUGHTS OF GREED AND EVIL, SO THAT HE WILL BE ABLE TO REACT SENSIBLY TO ANYTHING HE MEETS."   *(Karate saying)*

The syllable "Do" means "way" and can be found in other Japanese disciplines: Judo, Kendo, Aikido. Other martial arts use this syllable as a suffix like in "Karate-Do" In earlier times the martial arts were described with the suffix "Jutsu" (technique). Thus Kenjutsu and Karate-Jutsu were "Techniques with the sword" or "Techniques with the empty hand". According to the historical analysis by REILLY, this original suffix can be traced back to the necessity to use techniques, which, in extreme cases included self-defence. In Japan in the late 19th Century, this necessity was dying out. Various Kenjutsu schools organised competitions with the bamboo sword Shinai, which quickly gained popularity and led to the terminology Kendo. New social conditions and the changing way of life (in which the practice of the old Samurai arts took place) provided the background to the change of the original term from "Technique of the sword" to "Way of the sword". "Do" was meant to express the way to mastering the art. The term "Do" emphasised the continuous work regarding the psychological and physical requirements, the personality of the person training and fixed its aim on the target of improving the character and one's technical abilities.

SHOTOKAN KARATE

One important historical piece of background to this principle lies in Zen-Buddhism in Japan since the Kamakura period (1185-1333). The teaching of Zen-Buddhism can be attributed to the Indian monk BODIDHARMA. His religion, which spread quickly amongst the Samurai noble warlords, taught that the aim – the enlightenment (Satori) – could be induced and assisted by intensive bodily and spiritual meditation. Intensive forms of meditation lead from a (logical) thought process through to a vacuum and harmony between body and mind. Absolute obedience and the voluntary subjugation of the pupil to the instructions given by the Zen masters was a part of the religion. The Samurai practised a similar attitude to their feudal lords. Their moral code – called "Bushido" – bound them to absolute loyalty to the next upper-class above them. This loyalty went as far as the ritual suicide by falling on the sword. The "Seppuku" was the consequence for a Samurai who found he was not up to the task demanded of him.

The function of meditation was to place the Samurai into a state of inner peace, so that at the decisive moment, he was able to concentrate all his energy into one and overcome his fear of death. This demanded constant practice of the techniques and consequential work on his character traits. Perfection will never be achieved, but attempts will get close to it. Concentration and the ability to avoid obstructive feelings were the aim of meditation.

Transposed into the present day's Karate-Do, this would mean that it was not the perfection itself, which mattered, but the way towards it – practice. The techniques and the degree of mastering them are a reflection of the inner state of the body. "Mushin" – the art of freeing the mind – is there to help the pupil to go down this path. Although the precursors of Karate were the relatively "philosophy-free" fighting techniques originally stemming from the fishermen and farmers, the Japanese Karate masters gradually took up and included elements of Bushido and other forms, which had spiritual principles from Zen-Buddhism woven into Japanese society.

One relic from the strict hierarchy of Zen-Buddhism, that can be still found today in Karate and not prevalent in any other western sport system, is the hierarchical organisation of the sport by virtue of the grading system and the important role of the instructor – "Sensei". Also the rules of behaviour and the demand to go beyond training and master the art by constant practice throughout one's whole life can be traced back to the integration with Zen-Buddhism.

Numerous instructors of Karate on Okinawa had a code of morals. These were rules, that the Karateka was to hold himself to. These regulations – as "Doju-Kun" – are still used today in many extended versions. Here is the first written guide from the master SAKUGAWA (1733-1815):

- IMPROVE YOUR CHARACTER!
- MAINTAIN A CLEAN WAY OF LIVING!
- DEVELOP THE SENSE OF STRIVING!
- RESPECT OTHERS!
- REFRAIN FROM VIOLENT BEHAVIOUR!

The following rules by FUNAKOSHI are also an integral part of today's Karate ethics:

- NEITHER VICTORY NOR DEFEAT MAKE UP THE ULTIMATE AIM, RATHER THE IMPROVEMENT OF THE CHARACTER.
- IN KARATE THERE IS NO FIRST ATTACK.

The first sentence already makes it clear that Karate contains much more than only physical dimensions. Fighting spirit and the will to win should be brought alive by consequential training. However, training the mind, modesty, clean living and respect, self-control and good behaviour are equal and essential elements of Karate as well as the avoidance of force. The fact that there should be no first attack in Karate means that the Karateka may never provoke a fight. The gentleness and defensive characteristic of Karate is reflected in the Kata, which always start with a defensive technique.

The emblem for Shotokan Karate – the tiger in the circle – symbolises the aims of Karate-Do admirably. While the tiger symbolises the ability to fight and win, the circle round it symbolises a restriction of its freedom and its fighting spirit. The circle stands for reasonability, understanding, control and the spiritual principle of Karate-Do.

Today there are ritual and formal elements such as the bow of respect to the partner and the instructor at the beginning of routine daily training. Of course, they only represent the rudiments of the strict rules from the Samurai. In today's Dojo routine, they serve, however, as a sign of respect for one's fellow human beings and proof of good behaviour and self-control. The principles of the Do will always be expressed by the example shown by the instructor at the time. He has to assist the students in digging deeper into the depths of Karate. This cannot be achieved alone by the simple gaining of a belt grade. The training of the character and etiquette play their part since these also have a role in the perfection of the technique.

Mastering Karate has, nevertheless, an intermediate temporary form of success when one reaches the grade of first Dan. For those, however, who wish to improve and develop not only their technique but also their personality, the long road of Karate-Do will only just have begun.

THE DEMAND

2.1 Karate: Its Demands and Characteristics

2.1.1 The Basics

Most people take up Karate in order to learn self-defence. This is a legitimate reason and Karate offers a variety of possibilities to satisfy this personal requirement to strengthen the self-confidence and personal security, also mentally. Other motives, however, come quickly to the fore: to enjoy movement, to exercise the body, to find personal achievement, to experience an increase in the harmony of body and mind, to have companionship when training or gain sporting prowess and success in competition. The general and gradual improvement of techniques cannot be achieved in a few months or years alone, and will even stretch well over past the achievement of the first Dan. The benefits of personal and physical development will not only be present in the Dojo, they will also be a positive element of everyday life.

There are many millions of people who practice Karate despite the fact that Karate is still not an Olympic sport. The reason behind this lies in the variety of this sport – one of the most complex of all movement exercises. Apart from the spiritual and personal demands on the Karateka, he also trains his body in a very balanced manner. On the other hand, this kind of sport requires, from the beginning, a basic ability to be able to do motoric exercises. In Karate the whole of the body comes into play. As opposed to other sporting activities, Karate can be seen as a comprehensive sport from the physiological aspect. Providing one adapts to the main points of the training in the course of the years, this is why Karate can be something one does for the whole of one's life – right up until old age.

The basic abilities that one must have can be summarised into the following factors: stamina, speed, flexibility, coordination and power.

CHARACTERISTIC

2.1.2 Individual Karate Characteristics

In the main, text books express differing specific principles for Karate. The German Kata coach E. KARAMITSOS (5th Dan Shotokan) defines them into three rules in his book about the basics of Karate:

- THE TECHNIQUE OF ACCURACY
- USING THE HIPS CORRECTLY
- TENSION AND RELAXATION (KIME)

2.1.2.1 The Technique of Accuracy

The efficiency of a technique does not rest alone on the perfection of its execution. Above all one must learn to use it where it will land on the most vulnerable point of the opponent. Vital points or Atemi points are for example in the Jodan area, the temple, the chin, the carotid artery, the larynx, the nose and the eyes. It fits the terminology better and is more precise to speak of target points rather than target areas. Using the principle of target accuracy, even small weaker people are able to hold off or even take out the opponent with explosive speed and the right use of a technique.

One must take note of the exact target points not only in Kumite but also in Kihon. At the same time one must not miss the opportunity to instill in the student the appropriate technique of accuracy. The "appropriateness of the means" must be the maxim in a real live situation.

TRAINING

2.1.2.2 Using the Hips

The use of the hips is the main element of movement in Karate. Rotating the hips transmits the energy of the body movement to its extremities. Speed and effectiveness in the technique is heightened through this transmission of energy. The centre of balance – the Hara – is also switched by using the hips. The energy for the technique stems from this. As we will see later, the basis for the sequence of movements lies in the correct posture, stability while moving and while in the steady standing position.

2.1.2.3 Kime

Kime (the focus of the energy used), Kiai (the fighting cry) and correct breathing are the culminating points of the Karate technique. If everything is done correctly, the full effect will be achieved. Naturally this all depends on the correct execution of the technique.

Kime is defined as the shortest point in time in a technique, when the muscles are used explosively from a relaxed posture to their use on a target. Following this, the body is brought back immediately into a relaxed position, always taking care to note the requirement of Zanshin – defensive on-guard position. Throughout, breathing plays a supporting role. We breathe through the nose and the mouth at the same time. In Kime, the rapid expulsion of breathing out has an important function. When the full energy of the technique has been transmitted to the opponent, the fighting cry, also called "Kiai" is given to signal an expression of having imparted the spiritual transfer of energy as well as the will to win. Breath is expelled from the diaphragm and not only out of the throat or chest area. Of course, the Kiai is also used to intimidate the opponent.

2.2 Karate Training

2.2.1 Training

In training it is normal to wear a white "Karate-Gi", while for grading it is imperative. The Gi should be loosely fitted, but comfortable, i.e., not too tight nor too loose, not too long nor too short. Dependent on the structure of the material, the Gi should absorb sweat, thus avoiding it sticking to the body. The jacket is held together using a cotton coloured belt, showing the Karateka's degree of technical development in the grading system. No further clothing

equipment or protection is necessary for normal training. In training for Kumite and in contests, it is recommended that men wear a protective box and women a breast protector. In addition, a gum-shield and fist protectors are advisable to avoid injury. Jewellery and adornments should be removed before training and naturally prior to a contest, in order to minimise the risk of injury. For spectacle wearers, it is recommended that contact lenses are purchased in the long run, because, despite controls, there is always the possibility during exercises with a partner, that glasses will be dislodged.

In respect for the people you are training with, personal hygiene rules should be maintained. Washed hands and feet, short-cut finger and toe nails as well as a regularly washed clean Karate-Gi are the basics for taking part in training. Because Karate is carried out in bare feet with a partner, keeping to these rules goes without saying and is a sign of mutual respect.

2.2.2 The Greeting and Dojo Etiquette

Training always begins with the greeting. After lining-up at the beginning of the training session, all the students stand in a line in order of their belt grading, and on the command of the instructor kneel down. The command for this is Seiza. The signal for closing the eyes and beginning to concentrate on the training is Mokuso. Meditation is designed to clear the mind of everyday things and empty the inner body. Assuming a deliberate, regulated manner of breathing assists the aim of

WARMING UP

emptying the mind, getting ready for Karate and being open to whatever is going to happen. For the Mokuso phase after training, this is used to go over what has been learned and to relax.

Following on, there is then the traditional Shomeni-Rei. This is done by bowing forwards to the front and to the school as well as those who pass through. Sensei-ni Rei – the greeting towards the master – emphasises the respect and preparedness to follow his word during training and to concentrate and work hard during the training. Otagani-Rei is the command for ensuring politeness and consideration towards the other exercisers. Aggression should be banished and respect should take its place. Bowing to the partner should also impart a feeling to him to expect that fairness will be used in the upcoming contest. In any case, moreover, every Karateka is committed to helping the weaker one and not to place himself in the foreground. In practice, upholding etiquette rules varies from Dojo to Dojo. The important thing is, however, that the correct mental attitude is maintained.

2.2.3 Warming up and Gymnastics Exercises

Principle: The meaningful planning of training is necessary, not only for the individual session but also for the long-term training plan. Neither the karate-students nor the instructor will profit from improvised training, which has no clearly defined aim. With an eye on preparation for grading, it will be indispensable to concentrate on the exact content of the training session. The grading programme contains many important elements of Karate and, therefore, should always be a part of regular training.

After the greeting, training begins with a warming up and gymnastics phase. It is recommended that this should start with light exercises, so that energy reserves are not all used up already at the beginning of the session. Exercises to build up strength and power should be done at the end of the training session and not at the beginning. Remembering that a normal training session only lasts one and a half hours, and this at a frequency, normally, of only 2-3 times a week, the training session must always be planned and organised down to the last item. The trainer must take account of which group he is instructing – beginners, an older group, women, men or a mixed group, children, lower or upper grade? Each group requires a different approach to the aim of the training. The profile of the demands in the session must, of course, be relative to the degree of development of the participants.

WARMING UP

Since the main emphasis of every training session is always the practice of Karate techniques, warming up as well as aerobic exercises must have a direct bearing on the content of the training to follow. The corresponding exercises for the muscles and joints should be light and prepare one for the training. The principle of going from the simple to the complicated is valid here. The maxim for the trainer should be to use the time optimally so that the student's skills are improved. The rule for those being trained is – have patience! To learn Karate properly is a long road and takes continual, determined and concentrated training. One must always try to watch the instructor carefully and note how he demonstrates the movements and explains their execution. Self-criticism and the will to improve contribute just as much to progress as the correct methodology. Rather than attempting to execute a technique in a mechanical and powerful way, in certain circumstances it is better to first do it slowly, even if initially you do it wrongly, until it is then perfected. For help with this, there are valuable and useful aids such as textbooks or videos.

Warming up and aerobic exercises should never become a ritual. They should always aim to **prepare** you for Karate. This first part of a training session should be used directly for Karate. The following suggestion attempts to illustrate this.

Let us assume that the training session is to do with Kihon and Kumite. Simple sparring exercises (not actual fighting), using the more important individual techniques at the beginning, play an additional function to the main aim of warming up. They get the Karateka to practice his basic Karate skills – a feeling for space and speed of reaction. He learns to work at his coordination and fighting strategy in a stress-free and enjoyable manner that enables him to adjust to different opponents.

The specific execution of the Kumite technique (e.g., drawing the striking hand to the rear) can be practised early on here in conjunction with the basic techniques, which will be used in sparring or even contests. It is important that only the Gyaku-Zuki and Kizami-Zuki techniques should be used, which require no preparatory stretching exercises. In this phase, nor should there be hard blocks and only light Chudan contact, as well as no kicking movements, which require extensive stretching exercises (only use Chudan foot techniques), nor any other complicated combinations. The main thing is to exercise a loose but concentrated execution of the movements. During these exercises one should continually remain on the move, because the main aim of the first phase is to warm up. Here, the trainers must make sure that the correct way of doing the movements is carried out, just as much as during the Kihon, Kata and Kumite elements of the training.

KIHON

For the beginning of the stretching exercises, the maxim is to begin first when the body has been warmed up. Normally, this is when a thin film of sweat covers the body. If the illustrated partner exercises are carried out for 10-15 minutes, this will usually be the case. The muscles will then be supple enough to be able to be stretched. Aerobic exercises must also be well thought through. Care must always be taken to ensure that the exercises are safe and will not cause injury. The trainer must ensure he is 100% familiar with the up-to-date principles of functional gymnastics. About 15 minutes should be devoted to aerobic exercises before a Karate session. Specific preparatory stretching exercises can always be repeated during the remaining training.

At the end of the training session the strengthening exercise phase can be carried out. Press-ups and stomach and hip exercises – correctly carried out – are as always the commonest exercises to improve strength and develop power. Relaxation exercises can round the training off.

2.2.4 Kihon

The next phase – Kihon – should follow the didactical principle of "from the simple to the complicated"; individual techniques to start with, then combinations and foot techniques. The content should have the theme of building up to the grading programme. Let us assume that the trainer takes a regular group of grown-ups in the upper grade, and that on one day in the week the main emphasis is on Kihon. The following cycle of weeks is suggested: for example over a period of four weeks, the upper grade would train for the basic programme of the third Kyu to the first Dan during each session. In this way one is oriented towards the grading situation and can prepare oneself optimally for it by constant repetition. The first element should be carried out slowly in order to get used to the individual technique or combination demanded. The trainer can intervene to correct at this point. The second element follows with Kime and Kiai.

In order to progress, corrections given in the form of constructive encouragement are important for every person being trained. A good Karate instructor is able to spot a bad posture and mistakes in the movements being carried out and gives assistance and suggestions for improvement. It is recommended that every candidate asks his trainer prior to the grading test, what improvements are needed, so that these can be targeted well before the event.

One or two tips regarding the specific Karate and safe (from a health point of view) ways of carrying out the Kihon technique. One must always ensure that the movements are carried out in a controlled manner at all times. Beginners and students must rely on the trainer to lead them here, as they are often not in a position to realise this themselves. With Keri as well as with Zuki, the snap or braking movement finishes **before** the final stretching action. The spine should always be held straight, also in the elementary schooling, so that pressure is avoided in the hollow of the back. Men more likely than women to tend to hunch up their shoulders or adopt a cramped position. Here, tension is inherently transferred into the basic position, which is important (Kime) although it is only for the fraction of a second as the hit goes in. This makes the sequence of movements slow and incorrect. The last maxim is the gliding action moving forward. If the foot is lifted too high during the step forward, the result is a stamping effect, which costs time, places pressure on the knee joint and causes unnecessary noise.

2.2.5 Kumite

The different forms of Kumite, which are necessary to be demonstrated in the grading programme, make it essential that in the last phase of training, one or two of these forms should be practised thoroughly. It is always preferable to practice the complete Kumite sequence e.g., the Jiyu-Ippon, slowly first of all by numbers. If the elements of the technique are correct then one can increase the speed and carry the movement out with Kime and Kiai. Variations of counter-attack with the standard technique Gyaku-Zuki, can then be carried out as a counter with short techniques such as Empi, Hiza-Geri, Teisho etc.

Sparring can round off this type of training. The instructor must ensure that during this, no hard contact is made. Control is always the highest maxim in Kumite. Sometimes it is recommended that fighting partners are the same sex, dependent on how well the participants have developed their feeling for distance and fighting ability. An important aid to improving an individual's fighting ability is to watch good Karate competitors in action.

KATA

2.2.6 Kata

Many Dojos have separate Kata training. The training should be used not only to learn new Kata, but also used to carry out systematic revision of well-known practised Kata. The Kata represent the wealth of Karate – an enormous variety of otherwise little practised techniques. For this very reason training in them is very relevant.

It is often forgotten that the higher the aspired grading, the broader the spectrum and Karate repertoire have to be. The understanding of timing, coordination and the finer points should always be uppermost in the Karate training programme. In addition the purpose (application) of each of the techniques must be well understood. For this the instructor and the grading judge each have a partially different focus. Whether it is good sense to place Bunkai (Kata application) to the fore, as is the case often nowadays, is doubted by many, including traditional Karatekas. Many of the Kata techniques are of a symbolic nature or defensive and/or counter-measures against attacks carried out with the old Samurai weaponry or by Okinawan inhabitants. To organise Bunkai in such a loose manner that it turns into Kumite, is often practised as a new facet. Therefore, why not go directly for sparring? Good Kumite skills are much closer to the reality of the contest and self-defence. In my opinion, it is quite sufficient to know the most practical, contemporary Kata situations and occasionally practice them. Nevertheless, the schooling of the Kata sequences should remain in the forefront of training – flexibility, coordination, rhythm, the aesthetics of movement and finally fitness. Intensive Kata training is therefore indispensable. Without Kata, Karate-Do would be unthinkable.

2.3 Gradings

In most Karate Clubs or Unions the time taken to gain the next higher belt is laid down. Whatever length of time is considered to be the norm, it is always advisable to allow a month or two more between belt gradings, so that you can be sure that you are actually able to fulfil the technical requirements. At the beginning it is perfectly adequate to train twice a week. Since the degree of difficulty of the techniques to be demonstrated increases from Kyu grade to Kyu grade, it is advisable to increase the training rate in the later phases.

For example, in Germany, the minimum preparatory time for grown-ups is laid down as three months between grading tests up to the 6th Kyu. At least four months must elapse between the grading tests for the 5th Kyu and the 1st Kyu. The gap between the 1st Kyu and the 1st Dan must be at least a year.

It is necessary to really get to know the programme for the grading test – even better if you are able to learn the Kyu grade being aimed at off by heart. This is because you will go into the test fully knowing what is required. The student should obtain the official grading programme from the leader of the Dojo or instructor. It is also important to revise the Kihon and Kata sequences, not only during the training sessions but outside them, so that the techniques and sequences become second nature. The student, just as much as the Grader, must be clear what is expected of him in order to gain the next grade belt. So that both have the clearest possible picture of this, there are clear definitions in the programme of what has to be achieved and what is expected.

2.3.1 Lower Grades

In the *Lower Grades*, from *the 9th to the 7th Kyu*, the Karateka must be able to master the basics of the individual techniques. A firm posture, correct techniques and the reverse punch are important. An upright posture as well as being able to show the beginnings of the inner and external tensing of the limbs must all be evident. The controlled execution of the Kumite techniques as well as being able to keep one's distance are called for here. The sequence of the Kata must be correct and one must be able to demonstrate a good rhythm. The individual Kata techniques must be understood.

2.3.2 Middle Grades

In the *Medium Grades – 6th to 4th Kyu* – attention must be given to the perfection of the techniques. The quality of the individual technique must not suffer because the demonstration of the combinations has taken all the time up. Further criteria for Kihon are: the rhythm of the movements, deliberate use of the hips, a firm posture, breathing technique and Kime, the relaxed position at the end of the technique. In Kumite, the fluency of the movements, fighting spirit and control are now the important criteria to be judged. The Kata must be carried out flowingly and reflect that the meaning of the sequence of movements has been learned and understood.

UPPER GRADES

2.3.3 Upper Grades

The *Upper Grades – 3rd to 1st Kyu* – are characterised by the requirement of a higher technical level, which is expressed in the more difficult Kihon combinations. The quality of the individual techniques must not suffer as a result of the increased complexity. A firm posture, a flowing rhythm from one movement to the next, and, last not least, an improved physical condition are all demanded of the candidate. In Kumite sparring will now be included. Exact techniques, coupled with good fighting spirit and control are the main measures of the programme in this section. A victory or a defeat are not decisive factors for the grading test. In carrying out the Kata, an advanced understanding of the use of the movement should be demonstrated. The whole Kata repertoire comes now into play, because all Kata learned up until now can be tested.

The grading test for the 1st Dan, which is well above the technical standard for any earlier belt grading by virtue of its degree of difficulty, must demonstrate a maturity and exude the correct amount of style and execution in all parts of the test. It is this, which separates the Black belt from all the other grades.

Graders are often asked which area will be judged the strictest. Answers are legion. In principle the three areas – Kihon, Kata and Kumite – should be judged equally. However, if there are already significant mistakes in the first part of the test – the basic schooling – then the Kata and Kumite sections will probably not be considerably any better. It can, therefore, be assumed that a good performance in the basic schooling – the first impression that will be gained by the grader – generally indicates a good standard could be achieved throughout by the candidate. Graders also take other criteria into account such as age, constitution and the attitude shown by the candidate.

Of course, besides the necessary gap between gradings there are other *formal criteria* to take into account. The following are the more important ones:
Gradings can only be carried out by the holder of a valid grading licence for the particular style of Shotokan. The candidate must be in possession of a valid, up-to-date personal record card. Testing should not be carried out if this is not available. The candidate must have his grade properly recorded in his personal record and the fact must be reported to the appropriate Association.

SHOTOKAN KARATE

"The secret of Karate lies in the legs". This short, often repeated sentence underlines the importance of leg-work in good Karate techniques. Those who have seen top fighter Toni DIETL – the Kumite Trainer from the DKV (Deutsche Karate Verband (German Karate Association)) – in action, know very well what is meant. It is this ability to execute lightning changes of the centre of balance of the body and maintaining the correct fighting distance, thus allowing the fighter to carry out a flexible attack or avoid one, that must be concentrated on.

The main emphasis is the way the middle part of the body is deported, because in Kumite it is necessary to be able to react in a flexible manner. The rear leg is always slightly bent during the movement phase to permit any rapid change. This position is a mixture of the on-guard position from **Zenkutsu-Dachi** and **Fudo-Dachi**. This allows for the rapid alteration of the centre of balance according to the situation – onto the forward leg for an intended attack or onto the rear leg in defence or ready to counter-attack. Here, it is the sliding step Suri-Ashi that has to be mastered, so that quick changes in the distance to the opponent can be carried out.

Generally, low and high stances and short or long positions are all possible dependent on the fighting distance to be observed. A firm posture as well as a correct balance are important for every move – whether it be high or low, short or long, broad or narrow – so that you can react adequately and accordingly. In Karate, the elements that make up the good balanced entity are; body posture, position of the hips, where the feet are placed in relation to each other, the displacement of the body weight over the legs and the ability to tense the muscles.

In basic training one learns all the basic posture positions and develops an understanding for a secure stance, the maintenance of a firm base stances and the corresponding body deportment. The three most important basic stances in Shotokan are **Zenkutsu-Dachi, Kokutsu-Dachi** and **Kiba-Dachi** are comprehensively explained in the following sections. Tips are included, aimed at avoiding damage to ligaments, joints and the spine. Karate training strengthens the muscles. Incorrect execution of the movements can, in the course of time, lead to joints and ligaments being damaged.

In general the following detailed points are valid:
When carrying out a forward or rearward movement, bend the knees slightly, so that the height of the posture is maintained. The technique and the moment of

initiating the movement are always simultaneously carried out. At the moment the foot is placed down on the ground, the technique is brought into play. Don't let the upper body 'fall' into the movement or lean backwards. Make sure you always keep an upright posture. Let the feet slide over the floor when moving forwards. This ensures maximum stability in the posture at all times, and moreover your energy will not be wasted in correcting the up-down movement and will permit full concentration on the aim.

The glossary at the end of this book will aid readers, where necessary, to quickly find the meaning of the Japanese expressions used in the following texts.

3.1 Musubi-Dachi

The starting position at the beginning of training ready for the greeting bow. The heels are together and the feet point outwards at a 45° angle.

3.2 Hachi-Dachi

The ready position. The feet are apart at almost shoulder width. The knees are slightly bent. The body is concentrated but held relaxed. Feet are pointing slightly outwards. For Heiko-Dachi, which is almost an identical position, the feet are parallel. Hachi-Dachi and Heiko-Dachi belong to the same group of normal ready or starting positions (Shizentai), which are adopted before techniques in other positions are executed.

3.3 Zenkutsu-Dachi

The front stance. Best suited for the attack and hard, direct block. Using the forward step, a large distance can be covered. How low one stands is dependent on the body height. The lower the centre of balance, the better the stability and ability to develop power. The weight of the body is placed mainly (about 60-70%) over the forward leg. The position of the feet in the sideways axis is about hip width apart. In this way the rapid use of the hips can be carried out and ensures that despite the movement a good balance is maintained. The toes of both feet are pointing forwards. The feet must be kept firmly on the floor.

1

2

3

4

ZENKUTSU-DACHI

Avoid the following mistakes:

Make sure that the knee of the leading leg does not fall inwards or outwards, but is kept pointing forwards. Keep the rear foot pointing forwards and not pointing out to one side. When taking a step forward or rearwards, don't turn the forward foot outwards first of all, but bring it, and the weight of the body, over the foot, which is firmly pointing forwards. The upper body must remain straight. When stepping forwards stay at the same height and don't hollow the back. Don't stand too deeply or too stretched out.

- IN THE ATTACK, THE HIPS ARE POINTING HEAD-ON TOWARDS THE OPPONENT (SHOMEN).
- IN THE DEFENCE, THE HIPS ARE ANGLED AT 45° (HANMI).

3.4 Kokutsu-Dachi

The back stance. The knees are bent. The weight of the body is mainly centred (70%) over the rear leg. This position easily allows defensive movements to be carried out and by changing the centre of balance, this permits an immediate counter-attack to be made. In this position the feet are at right angles to each other. The hips are angled 45° to the opponent.

Avoid the following mistakes:
Hold the back and the pelvis up straight and avoid hollowing the back (can lead to bringing the wrong stress onto the spine as a result). Watch the position of the rear bent leg. It should not be allowed to wander inwards, but should be positioned over the foot and show a slight tension outwards. The front leg should not be stretched out.

1

2

3

4

3.5 Kiba-Dachi

The sideways position (sometimes called the 'horse stance'). Particularly suited for the execution of sideways aimed kicks or short arm movements. The weight of the body is maintained exactly in the middle of the body. The feet are parallel and the knees bent. The leg muscles are tensed outwards. The back is held straight in order to avoid it becoming hollowed. The stomach and buttock muscles are tensed.

Avoid the following mistakes:
Don't allow the upper body to dip forwards or backwards – keep it upright. Don't stand with a hollowed back. When moving, don't lift the centre of balance, keep the legs bent instead. Don't allow the knees to 'fall' inwards.

FUDO-DACHI

3.6 Fudo-Dachi

Firm posture. The knees are bent and 60% of the weight of the body is centred over the forward leg. Using this strong position you can defend quickly and counter-attack. Sochin-Dachi is another expression used for this position.

3.7 Neko-Ashi-Dachi

Cat stance. Just like the Sanchin-Dachi, this position permits a firm stance when fighting at close quarters. About 85% of the weight of the body is centred over the rear leg. Both legs are bent. The forward foot is pointing forwards and touches the ground only with the ball of the foot. The sole of the rear foot is placed flat on the floor.

3.8 Jiyu-Dachi

Fighting position. The rear leg is slightly bent and the centre of balance is held a little higher than in the other positions. The arms should be held in front of the upper part of the body so that a defensive as well as an attacking movement is possible without having to move too far. The elbows should not protrude from the body, but held close to it to allow the arm technique to benefit from the impulse of the hips as they are brought quickly and directly onto the target.

DEFENCE/BLOCKS

Kihon – the training for basic techniques – constitutes the main element of any training. Constant training over a number of years will school precision and self-assurance. On the one hand the muscles will be strengthened by constant repetition. On the other hand, the Karateka will learn the accuracy of the techniques, without which successful results in neither Kata nor Kumite will be achieved.

At this juncture, the most important techniques will be illustrated and described. The instructions, on how to execute them, will help in perfecting them. Without good individual techniques, good combinations will not be possible. Again the general principle is valid: practice slowly and accurately until the individual parts of the movement are coordinated correctly.

Working at the full speed comes only after this stage has been reached. The basic techniques that follow are only a selection of the full Karate repertoire, but they are the most common ones.

General Tips for Training in the Basic Techniques

When executing the forwards or rearwards movement don't tip the upper body backwards. The back remains straight and the shoulders are always held loosely. For defensive techniques and attacks with the fist it is important that the end of the arm movement and the end of the foot movement are timed to be simultaneous.

The fist should hit the target at the same moment as the forward foot is set down. The tension of the body is at its greatest at the end of the technique – breathe out at this point. If the sequence of the technique is in order, then the movements should be carried out fluently and quickly. The point to watch for is that the hips are used correctly simultaneously to the movement being executed.

This is because the hips are the trigger to the acceleration of all the techniques. Keep an eye on the Hikite movements. The pulling back of the arm not being used in the attack gives the initial dynamic impulse. The arm that has been pulled back should not be raised up and outwards and the elbows point rearwards with the fist lying firmly against the waist.

When moving forward the weight of the body stays at the same height. This means you have to avoid an up and down movement. To do this the knees are always slightly bent when moving forward.

AGE-UKE

4.1 Defensive Techniques/Blocks

Defensive techniques are the deeply rooted ones in the basic techniques. In Karate, as coined in the expression, the principle of a first strike is not accepted, and accordingly blocking gains an important role. They are almost always carried out using the arms. Blocking can be carried out with vigour, so that the attack is stemmed as soon as it begins and without a counter-attack.

When training without a partner, this should be remembered, so that the execution of a block can be consequentially performed. On the other hand, when blocks are being practised with a partner in training, evasive actions and precise execution, bearing in mind the safety of the partner's joints, can be included. The force applied by the attacker can thus be deflected by twisting the hips and using the correct direction for the block.

Note the following:
Don't block the attacking partner in his elbow joint area with your arm, as this can lead to injury. Always block using the soft part on the underside of your arm – don't use "bone on bone". Defend attacks using leg techniques so that the attacker's tendons and joints are not damaged, but instead block against the muscles. One should always execute a defensive movement quickly and then immediately follow on into a counter-attack.

For this you turn the hips into the Hanmi position (45° angle). In this way you narrow the target danger zone offering only a small attack area and are ready to tense for the counter-attack movement. It is important to maintain the correct distance between yourself and your partner when carrying out any of the blocks.

4.1.1 Age-Uke

A rising defensive block. Age-Uke is mostly used as a block against Oi-Zuki Jodan. However, it can also be used as a direct attack against the neck or chin. Used as a block, Age-Uke deflects the attack upwards. At the last phase in the movement, the forearm should be snapped upwards.

AGE-UKE

UCHI-UKE

The shoulder on the side of the arm effecting the block is kept down. It is moved upwards in front of the body. The back of the fist and the forearm lie in a straight line. Correct braking effect in the end phase. Watch out for the Hikite movement of the other arm. The distance between the arm and the forehead is about two fist widths.

4.1.2 Uchi-Uke

'Inner' block. The backwards movement of the defending arm under the other one determines how quickly the defence can be effected. In the Uchi-Uke it is important that the arm always comes flush with the side of the body.

The fist must be at shoulder height in the final phase. The elbow is drawn almost into the body, but still stays about one fist width away from the waist. At the moment the snap movement of the forearm is done, the hips are twisted round. During this don't hold the defending arm too close to the body.

As a general rule this type of block is used to ward off attacks against the centre of the body. Uchi-Uke can also be used as a Jodan blocking technique against attacks to the head and neck.

UCHI-UKE

1

2

3

4

5

6

4.1.3 Soto-Uke

Outward block. The backwards movement takes place at head height with the back of the fist pointing forwards. The back of the fist being pulled back points to the rear as the arm is brought backwards.

The other arm is brought slowly forwards in the direction of the opponent, and, when executing the defensive movement, it is whipped sharply backwards simultaneously with the twist of the hips and commencement of the block. The shoulders are held at the same height.

The defending arm is brought forward. The end of this phase is when it is in front of the body so that the whole of the rib-cage is protected. At the end of the movement the fist is at about shoulder height with the arm angled at about 90º and the elbows are pointing downwards.

Don't hold the defending arm too close to the body.

SOTO-UKE

1

2

3

4

5

6

GEDAN-BARAI

4.1.4 Gedan-Barai

Blocking an attack with a downwards sweeping movement. The defending arm is brought from the side of the face. At the same time the other arm is pointing downwards.

As already described in the other defensive techniques illustrated, Gedan-Barai also gets its power and dynamics from the simultaneous twisting movement of the hips and the snapping back of the other arm.

In the end phase, the defending fist is directly over the forward knee. You use this technique to ward off fist attacks or kicks aimed at the lower abdomen region.

GEDAN-BARAI

1

2

3

4

5

6

4.1.5 Shuto-Uke

Defence to the side. Shuto means "sword" and is carried out with the open hand. This movement is carried out from close to the head. The inside of the hand points towards the face. The opposite arm is stretched out in the pull back phase and the elbow of the arm being pulled back is pointed slightly downwards.

Shuto-Uke is different from the other techniques described so far, in so much that the main characteristic of the pulled back arm with the open hand is that it stops at the height of the solar-plexus and not at the side of the body.

When doing the Shuto-Uke, the Kokutsu-Dachi stance is mainly adopted with the weight of the body centred over the rearward leg. The point with this movement is that it is a difficult defensive technique and demands a lot of practice.

The principles of striking, Hikite, use of the hips, turning the forearm (here it is the edge of the hand) at the last moment in carrying out the movement are all identical, however, with those of the other blocks.

In order to be able to do the movement correctly, it is imperative that the forward arm is not stretched out and that the back of the hand forms a straight line with the forearm.

SHUTO-UKE

1

2

3

4

5

6

4.2   Attack Techniques Using the Arms

The different types of thrusts or strikes to be used are dependent on the distance to be covered. In addition to the features of the basic postures and techniques, described already, which you have to watch to make sure you carry them out properly, there are some more points that must be treated the same way.

The classic Karate attacking techniques using the arms usually comprise straight stabs in a forwards direction. A precise aiming point and the correct range now play an important role in order to be able to execute the technique and stop the movement, down to the last millimetre, before it hits the target.

The striking surface consists always of the knuckles of the fore and middle fingers. As the fist is accelerated forwards, it must always be squeezed together tightly.

4.2.1 Oi-Zuki

Straight fist punch. The Oi-Zuki fist punch has a number of advantages. First of all it permits fighting at distance because of its enormous range, and secondly it develops a great deal of force against the opponent, because of the employment of the whole of the body.

For it to be efficient, the following principles must be observed: keep the centre of balance low and during the movement always keep it at the same height. In the end phase of the Oi-Zuki the upper body and the pelvis are frontal to the opponent. The whole of the soles of both feet are flat on the floor.

OI-ZUKI

4.2.2 Gyaku-Zuki

Reverse punch. The use of this one in Kumite is very varied. Whether as a counter-attack, a direct counter-attack or attack, as an individual technique or in combination with another movement, Gyaku-Zuki is an extremely versatile and powerful technique. Gyaku means having one foot forward as the strike comes from the opposite side of the body.

Used in conjunction with stepping forward movements (Suri-Ashi), large distances can be covered when fighting. At the beginning of the movement the rear leg is slightly bent.

In the final phase, the pelvis twists round to end up frontally to the opponent as the leg is stretched. The same principles regarding the basic posture apply as in Oi-Zuki. The correct, rapidly executed use of the hips makes the Gyaku-Zuki a very dangerous, powerful technique.

GYAKU-ZUKI

1

2

3

4

5

4.2.3 Kizami-Zuki

Short punch. Kizami-Zuki is carried out at short distance to the opponent in a rapid and explosive manner. It begins from the Kamae start position without pulling back the strike arm, before punching.

Usually you glide quickly forward at the same time into the target. The shoulders and the axis of the hips are at 45°.

When doing the movement in basic training, the technique goes as far as a fixed point and the pupil returns dynamically back into the Kamae position.

The Kizami-Zuki is not as powerful as the Oi-Zuki or the Gyaku-Zuki, but nevertheless it can work as a good surprise technique without the requirement for any preparatory movement.

4.2.4 Uraken-Uchi

Uraken is a punching technique. The arm, which is executing the punch, is moved in a half-circular motion aimed at the side of the opponent's head e.g., the temple or the neck artery (carotid).

To do the Uraken, the pull back must be correctly carried out in a whiplash type of action of the forearm before the arm and elbow joint is fully stretched forward.

You can also execute the Uraken as a downwards movement (Tate-Uraken), but the quickest variant is the punching technique described above (Yoko-Uraken).

4.2.5 Empi-Uchi

The elbow attack. Empi is a close-quarters fighting technique and is executed in various ways: Mae-Empi (straight), Yoko-Empi (to the side), Tate-Empi (upwards), Otoshi-Empi (downwards), Ushiro-Empi (from the turn) and Yoko-Mawashi-Empi (circular sideways)

By virtue of the use of the hips, the Empi is a very effective technique for self-defence over short distances. In contests or when sparring, this technique should not be used because there is a high danger of injury being caused.

Photos Page 67:
1. *Mae-Empi (straight)*
2. *Yoko-Empi (to the side)*
3. *Tate-Empi (upwards)*
4. *Otoshi-Empi (downwards)*
5. *Ushiro-Empi (from the turn) and*
6. *Yoko-Mawashi-Empi (circular sideways)*

EMPI-UCHI

4.2.6 Shuto-Uchi

The 'sword-hand' or edge of the hand punch. The way the hand is held is the same as in Shuto-Uke. The striking arm is thrust forward from the outside or from the inside of the body. Suto-Uchi comes in numerous variations mainly in Kata and Kihon. It is hardly ever used in Kumite. Just like all the Karate techniques, the full use of the hips will guarantee the execution of an efficient technique.

Uchi Mawashi Uchi (from the inside to the outside)

Haito Uchi (using the thumb side edge of the hand)

Soto Mawashi Uchi (from the outside to the inside)

4.3   Attack Techniques Using the Legs

The big advantage of techniques using the foot, if executed correctly, lies in the enormous power developed by the movement. You can summon up more power with your legs than with your arms. In addition you can use foot techniques harmlessly to bridge large distances or to hold the opponent off. You can use kicks in all possible directions.

On the other hand they require more time in their preparation and training. You can learn how to move your arms more quickly and easily than your feet, since you always use your hands for a variety of reasons and rarely your feet.

Poorly executed foot techniques can rapidly bring the Karateka into a difficult spot, even in a self-defence situation, because he can easily lose his balance and quickly become a victim of his opponent. In order to avoid making mistakes, it is useful to visualise the kicking movements in phases. If one part of the movement is done wrongly, the kick loses its effect and is more dangerous for the person carrying out the kick than for the opponent.

Watch out for the following basic principles:
Without the correct start there will be no correct technique. Watch out for the correct starting position of the attacking knee. The knee of the kicking leg must be bent and lifted up high during the preparatory phase, while the heel is held as close as possible to the standing leg. The standing leg is always bent.

When executing the sideways kick the standing leg turns with the kick. The kick itself is a whiplash movement. Always start off by mastering a good Chudan technique before going on to target the head region. During all the whiplash foot techniques (Keage), bring back the lower leg in a snapping movement and do this before the leg is fully stretched out. When kicking, you must keep your balance.

Don't make 'rowing' movements with your arms during the kick, instead maintain a good Kamae position. The upper body remains upright and must not fall backwards or forwards (hollowed back). The feet must be in the correct position and the ankle is tensed. The technique ends when the foot is put down again. Here, you must take care to put the leg down in a controlled and deliberate manner.

MAE-GERI

4.3.1 Mae-Geri Keage

Straight kick forwards. The Mae-Geri gets its effect from the whipping movement of the lower leg and the impulse of a simultaneous thrusting forwards of the hips. First of all the start is correctly positioned: the kicking leg is pulled up close to the rear of the thigh.

Now the foot whips forward in a direct continuous, flowing movement. At the end of this, the lower leg is immediately and rapidly whipped back and finally set down quietly and firmly. The tip of the foot (toes) is lifted up and you punch with the ball of the foot. Just like all the other kicks, Chudan or Jodan are possible target areas.

In the less common version Mae-Geri Kekomi, the kicking leg is stretched out at the end of the movement and stopped so that the punch is done with the heel. Mae-Geri can be done with the forward leg as well as with the rearward leg.

1   2

MAE-GERI

3

4

5

6

7

YOKO-GERI

4.3.2   Yoko-Geri

Sideways kick. The Kekomi version differs from Keage (whip kick) in the starting position and the end phase of the movement. At the beginning of doing the Kekomi, the knee is brought up high. The leg then stretches out with a short stopping distance and the punch is carried out using the side edge of the foot or the heel. The impulse of the hips is in the direction of the kick.

For Keage, when starting the movement, the leg is not brought up quite so high, but rather more left at an angle of 45º to the direction of the kick. The Keage is whipped back quickly and a short impulse with the hips adds to the power of the technique. Both Yoko-Geri variations are generally executed in the Kiba-Dachi position. For this, the position of the foot at the start is parallel to the ground and the toes are angled upwards.

It is now important that the standing leg remains bent in order to allow you to retain your balance when you hit the target. When moving on from Kiba-Dachi, you must take care to ensure that the axis of the hips remains parallel to the ground and doesn't get tipped over when starting.

Photos on the left: Yoko-Geri Kekomi
Photos on Page 69: Koko-Geri Keage

YOKO-GERI

1

2

3

4

5

6

MAWASHI-GERI

4.3.3 Mawashi-Geri

Roundhouse kick. This action is carried out with an arching movement, which is different from all the straight kicking actions. The strength of this kick is achieved by a rapid twisting of the hips and the whipping motion in its final phase. You can get round the opponent's guard with the Mawashi-Geri, especially when a direct line isn't available, and this turns it into a very efficient weapon.

The way it is executed in basic training is always by using the ball of the foot as the striking surface. In Kumite you use the instep. At the start, the knee should always point slightly upwards. The heel should be pulled close to the rear side of the thigh, in order to create the situation for an efficient whipping movement.

After the rotation of the body, the leg strikes the target horizontally. After this, the leg is snapped back at the same level, and only then is it followed by deliberately setting it down. The hips are brought back into the starting position.

1   2

MAWASHI-GERI

3

4

5

6

7

8

4.3.4 Ushiro-Geri

Back kick rearwards. This technique is executed by using the heel following a twist of the hips. The forward leg is the standing leg and the rear leg is distinctly angled, and after a 180° turn, it is stretched out towards the opponent. As soon as the action is started, you must line up your aim on your opponent over your shoulder.

After stretching out the leg and landing on target, it is brought back at the same level, and only then do you turn back forward again. At the end phase the hips are locked momentarily. At all costs, the standing leg in this technique must not be stretched out, otherwise you will lose your balance. The upper body is now leaning slightly forward in order to avoid hollowing the back.

The commonest mistake is to put too much effort into the turning around phase. If you do this the turning movement of the hips will be uncontrollable.

1   2

USHIRO-GERI

3

4

5

6

7

4.3.5 Ura-Mawashi-Geri

Roundhouse with the heel or sole of the foot. Ura-Mawashi-Geri can be done using the forward or rear leg. Just like Mawashi-Geri, this action is carried out with an arching movement and allows you to get round the opponent's guard. In contests you use the sole of the foot to strike with, while in self-defence you use the heel. Once again, the start plays a large, decisive part for success in this technique.

The start is similar to a Yoko-Geri from the Zenkutsu-Dachi position. Then, by using the hips and a slight twist of the standing foot, you strike to the head.

After the strike lands at the side of the head, the leg and the hips are immediately brought back into a normal position. Using Ura-Mawashi in combat demands enormous agility and speed.

1   2

URA-MAWASHI-GERI

KUMITE

5.1 Kumite

This chapter describes the various basic forms of training with a partner. The maxim of Kumite training is "from the simple to the complex". This means that you should learn the simple forms of Gohon-Kumite first of all in order to internalise the way of keeping your distance when attacking and defending as well as counter-attacking. Only then should you go on to practice further Kumite based variations such as Kihon-Ippon, Kaeshi-Ippon and Jiyu-Ippon. In order to gain the most out of Kumite training, you must master the basic positions and techniques. These exercises with a partner, which are laid down and also are demanded in Kyu grading, are carried out technically in the form of Kihon. In other words, up to Jiyu-Ippon Kumite, just as in basic schooling, you should halt the attack, block and counter, and in the final phase of the technique achieve a full Kime. The Kumite variants are carried out directly from the basic position Zenkutsu-Dachi without a step forward action.

Supporting exercises are included for every stage of basic training right up to free fighting situations for the Kumite form. They require more agility in the preparatory phase of the attack or counter-attack. In these actions, the movement is snapped back at the end of the motion like in Randori or Jiyu-Kumite. At the end of this chapter you will find numerous tips and examples for free fighting, which are useful in contests and also in Jiyu-Kumite.

GOHON-KUMITE

5.1.1 Gohon Kumite

The attacker stands with his left leg forwards in a Zenkutsu-Dachi position and he carries out a Oi-Zuki Jodan five times (the illustration shows only three attacks). On the last attack he ends it with a Kiai. The defender stands in a Heiko-Dachi position and then takes a step backwards with the left foot and defends with an Age-Uke. At the fifth attack he makes a Gyaku-Zuki counter-attack ending it with a Kiai. Both return to the Shizentai position and the other partner carries out an Oi-Zuki Jodan. At the end of this, the original attacker carries out an Oi-Zuki Chudan five times ending the last one with a Kiai. The defender takes a step back with the left foot again and blocks using a Soto-Uke. After the last block he counter-attacks with a Gyaku-Zuki, ending with a Kiai.

1   *2*   *3*

4   *5*   *6*

First Sequence

6 a

GOHON-KUMITE

7

8

9

10

Second Sequence

GOHON-KUMITE

Notes on Gohon Kumite and Sanbon Kumite

Gohon Kumite is the basic form of the exercises with a partner. The prearranged training of attack and defence situations, using simple techniques, is the basic element of learning the Kumite sequences. The aims are: to get the feeling for keeping your distance, control, fighting spirit, as well as developing a feeling for the right attack and defence situation.

It is assumed that the techniques of basic training for this type of exercise have already been learned. The difference between Gohon Kumite and Sanbon Kumite lies in the number of techniques demanded, as well as the starting position of the attacker and defender.

Initially, both partners stand opposite each other in the Shizentai posture. The greeting follows and then the attacker takes stock of the right distance between the partners. He then takes a step backwards with the right foot into the Zenkutsu-Dachi position and executes a Gedan-Barai.

The announcement is made whether the attack phase is to be for a Jodan or a Chudan. The attack is then carried out 5 times with the last one ending with a Kiai. The defender retreats each time with his defence blocks.

After the fifth attack, the defender makes a counter-attack with a Gyaku-Zuki ending with a Kiai. After this the attacker moves backwards with his forward leg and the defender brings his rearward leg forward. The exercise is ended with the formal bow.

In Gohon Kumite, the main things to watch for are the posture and the precise execution of the techniques. Both partners must concentrate on carrying out the movements as learned in the Kihon training.

Besides maintaining a firm standing position and good deportment of the body (don't lean forwards or backwards during the movement), it is crucial not to 'race' through the movement techniques. On the contrary, each phase must be consequentially carried out before the next one is started.

The safety of your partner and consideration of his ability is very important in all Kumite forms.

GOHON-KUMITE

KUMITE
Gohon Kumite
This is the same as for the 9th Kyu with the only difference being that the defender moves his right leg backwards on the first defensive movement.

This creates a mirror image situation.

1

2

3

4

5

First Sequence

GOHON-KUMITE

6

7

8

9

10

Second Sequence

SANBON-KUMITE

KUMITE
Sanbon-Kumite
This is the same as for the 9th Kyu, however, the attack is only carried out three times. The Kiai follows the third attack, i.e., block or counter to it.

In addition you must attack with a Mae-Geri and the defence responds with a Nagashi-Uke and a step backwards. The defender uses his left leg to do this, while the attacker takes a step forward with his right leg from a left footed Zenkutsu-Dachi.

After the third Nagashi-Uke, a counter-attack with a Gyaku-Zuki is made, ending with a Kiai.

1   2   3

4   5

5.1.2 Kihon Ippon Kumite

The attacker stands alternately once with the left leg forward, and once with the right leg forward in the Zenkutsu-Dachi position. From this position he executes two attacks (for each position i.e., left leg or right leg) using Oi Zuki at the Jodan region, Oi Zuki at the Chudan region and Mae-Geri (a total of six attacks). The defender moves from the Shizentai position backwards, always using the right leg and employs the following defensive techniques: Age-Uke twice and Soto-Uke twice. For the Mae-Geri attack he goes backwards first of all with the right leg and dodges into a 45° angled Zenkutsu-Dachi position and uses a Gedan-Barai.

At the second attack he dodges left in a 45° angled Kokutsu-Dachi position and uses a Nagashi-Uke. After each block, the counter-attack Gyaku-Zuki is used (six blocks, six counter-attacks).

1
2
3
4
First Sequence

KIHON-IPPON KUMITE

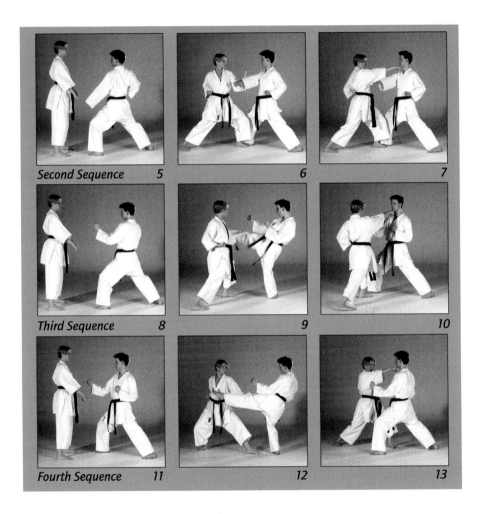

Second Sequence   5   6   7

Third Sequence   8   9   10

Fourth Sequence   11   12   13

KIHON-IPPON KUMITE

Notes on Kihon-Ippon Kumite

Basically the Kihon-Ippon Kumite is the same as the Gohon Kumite, only now every attack is blocked and a counter-attack delivered. Kihon means 'basic schooling' and Ippon means 'once', and this is exactly how the exercise form should be used. After the attacker returns into a Zenkutsu-Dachi position with a Gedan-Barai, there will then be an attack, as per the basic schooling while remaining in your position and before you go back after a few seconds using Zanshin (watching out for any individual action). Attacker and defender both return to their starting position after each of the actions. The attack and the counter-attack are both ended off with a Kiai. The counter-attack is carried out as per the basic schooling using Hikite with the other arm, coming to a braked stop at the end of the movement. For an attack with a Mae-Geri, a blocking technique with a dodge to the side should be used.

Sparring with a partner

Both Karateka stand opposite each other in the Kamae position. One stands with either the left or the right side forward and the other Karateka with the same side forward. The attack is carried out from the Zenkutsu-Dachi position using a Kizami-Zuki and Suri-Ashi at the Jodan region. It is defended from the Kokutsu-Dachi position using a Te-Nagashi-Uke and Suri-Ashi. The counter-attack is carried out using a Gyaku-Zuki at the Chudan region.

SPARRING EXERCISES

1

2

3   *First Sequence*

4

5

6   *Second Sequence*

SPARRING EXERCISES

Notes on exercising with a sparring partner

Sparring, using simple techniques, will prepare the Karateka for free fighting. Part of this is all to do with a good understanding for the execution of techniques from the Chudan Kamae position, the whipping back in the Gyaku-Zuki when counter-attacking and the perfection of techniques whilst on the move. The dodging movement or rapid gliding in Suri-Ashi and defence with the open hand are both elements to be included in training.

After moving back from the counter-attack you must deliberately adopt the Kamae position again. 'Deliberately' means that after the action you do not simply let your arms drop. On the contrary, you bring them back into the starting position again in a concentrated, tensed gliding motion.

Each technique is announced by the attacker. Each attack or counter-attack is ended with a shout of Kiai.

KAESHI-IPPON KUMITE

5.1.2 Kaeshi - Ippon Kumite

The attacker stands in a Zenkutsu-Dachi position, once with his left leg forward and once with his right leg forward. The defender stands in the Kamae position each time with the opposite leg.

First Sequence
Attack with an Oi Zuki at the Jodan region, defence is Age-Uke, with a step backwards. Then counter-attack with an Oi-Zuki at the Jodan region. The first attacker takes a step backwards, blocks with an Age-Uke and counter-attacks with a Gyaku-Zuki.

Second Sequence
Attack with an Oi-Zuki at the Chudan region, defence is Soto-Uke, with a step backwards. Then counter-attack with an Oi-Zuki at the Chudan region. The first attacker takes a step backwards, blocks with a Soto-Uke and counter-attacks with a Gyaku-Zuki.

Third Sequence
Attack with a Mae-Geri at the Chudan region, defence is Nagashi-Uke, with a step backwards. Then counter-attack with a Mae-Geri at the Chudan region. The first attacker takes a step backwards, blocks with a Nagashi-Uke and counter-attacks with a Gyaku-Zuki.

Sparring with a partner for free fighting
An attack is carried out three times from the Hidari-Kamae (starting position with left leg forward) and three times from the Migi-Kamae (starting position with the right leg forward).

Both stand in the Kamae position with the left foot forward and then with the right foot forward. Attack with a Gyaku-Zuki using Suri-Ashi at the Jodan region, final position Zenkutsu-Dachi. Defence is Soto-Uke, side dodge (Sabaki at a 45º angle) using Suri-Ashi to a Kokutsu-Dachi. Then comes the counter-attack with a Gyaku-Zuki at the Chudan region or Uraken.

KAESHI-IPPON KUMITE

1

2

3

4

First Sequence

KAESHI-IPPON KUMITE

5

6

7   *Second Sequence*

8

9

10   *Third Sequence*

KAESHI-IPPON KUMITE

Exercises for partners - sparring

Notes on Kaeshi-Ippon Kumite 1

The Kaeshi Ippon Kumite sequence is attack, block, counter-attack, block and counter, each time with a separate technique. The concept of stepping back immediately after an attack, as well as reacting by carrying out a counter-attack at the same time as taking one step forward after a block, should become second nature.

The partners stand opposite each other in a Chudan-Kamae position. The attacker starts a strong attack, which keeps the opponent in check so that he cannot immediately respond with a counter-attack. As a result the defender must back away and then takes one step forward again to carry out the counter-attack.

Now the attacker takes one step back, defends and counters. The Karateka must pause and hold his position for a short period in the end phase of both the attack and the counter-attack movement. In these preparatory exercises for free fighting, the main thing is to learn how to get the right timing for the counter-attack.

The basic forms of Gohon Kumite and Kihon Ippon Kumite must be mastered before you train in these variations. Carrying out the techniques and position must be done as per the basic training.

KAESHI-IPPON KUMITE

KUMITE
Kaeshi - Ippon Kumite 2

The attacker stands in a Kamae position, once with his left leg forward and once with his right leg forward. The defender stands in the Kamae position.

First Sequence
Attack with an Oi Zuki at the Jodan region, defence is Age-Uke, with a step backwards. Then counter-attack with an Oi-Zuki at the Chudan region. The first attacker takes a step backwards, blocks with a Soto-Uke and counter-attacks with a Gyaku-Zuki.

Second Sequence
Attack with an Oi-Zuki at the Chudan region, defence is Soto-Uke, with a step backwards. Then counter-attack with a Mae-Geri at the Chudan region. The first attacker takes a step backwards, blocks with a Nagashi-Uke and counter-attacks with a Gyaku-Zuki.

Third Sequence
Attack with a Mae-Geri at the Chudan region, defence is Gedan-Barai, with a step backwards. Then counter-attack with an Oi-Zuki at the Jodan region. The first attacker takes a step backwards, blocks with an Age-Uke and counter-attacks with a Gyaku-Zuki.

KAESHI-IPPON KUMITE

1

2

3

4

First Sequence

KAESHI-IPPON KUMITE

5

6

7 *Second Sequence*

8

9

10 *Third Sequence*

SPARRING EXERCISE

Sparring with a partner for free fighting

Both partners stand with either the left foot forward or the right foot forward. Attack with a Mae-Mawashi-Geri using the gliding step Suri-Ashi at the Jodan or Chudan region, final position Zenkutsu-Dachi. Defence is a Te-Nagashi-Uke backwards with a side dodge Sabaki at a 45° angle to the attack, using Suri-Ashi to a Kokutsu-Dachi. Then comes the counter-attack with a Gyaku-Zuki at the Chudan region or Uraken.

Sparring with a partner for free fighting

JIYU-IPPON KUMITE

5.1.2 Jiyu - Ippon Kumite

All the attacks occur twice, each time from the Kamae position. Which side leads is open to the partners. The attack techniques are Oi-Zuki at the Jodan region, Oi-Zuki at the Chudan region, Ushiro-Geri at the Chudan region and Mawashi-Geri. The defence and counter-attack techniques can be chosen freely, but the Suri-Ashi (gliding step) and the Kai-Ashi (step) must be used in combination with the movement chosen. The snapping back technique is used with the counter-attack followed then by gliding backwards into the Chudan Kamae position.

First Sequence

JIYU-IPPON KUMITE

5

6   *Second Sequence*

7

8   *Third Sequence*

9

10   *Fourth Sequence*

JIYU-IPPON KUMITE

11   12   *Fifth Sequence*

13   14   *Sixth Sequence*

15   16   *Seventh Sequence*

JIYU-IPPON KUMITE

17   18   *Eighth Sequence*

19   20   *Ninth Sequence*

SPARRING EXERCISE

Sparring with a partner for free fighting
First Sequence
Both partners stand with either the left foot forward or the right foot forward. Attack with a Kizami-Zuki using the gliding step Suri-Ashi at the Jodan region, final position Zenkutsu-Dachi. Defence is a De-Ai using Te-Nagashi-Uke and Gyaku-Zuki at the Chudan region.

Second Sequence
The Karateka adopt a mirrored starting position. Attack with Uraken at the Jodan region. Defence is a De-Ai using Te-Nagashi-Uke and Gyaku-Zuki at the Chudan region.

First Sequence   1   2   3

Second Sequence   4   5   6

JIYU-IPPON KUMITE

Notes on Jiyu Ippon Kumite

This Kumite form is very close to free fighting. Free fighting is learned in easy-to-grasp and predetermined sequences. Above all, in the sequences the defender is encouraged to use his reflexes to produce specific fighting actions.

Nevertheless, the individual techniques should follow the perfection of the basic training learned in relation to attacks and blocks. Blocks should be stopped short in the final end phase of the movement. On the other hand the counter-attack is immediately drawn back just like in free fighting. Just as in all the sparring sessions with a partner, attacks are always clearly announced beforehand.

Both partners adopt the basic position Chudan-Kamae. They must show that they have learned to be able to move from this position and gain a favourable advantage by attacking or by blocking and counter-attacking. The defender must make it possible that the attacker is able to act from the correct distance. After each action, the partners separate from each other, but remain in the Kamae position. The point to watch here now is the effectiveness and control of the counter-attack.

This must be shown to come from a perfect distance between the partners and prove that, in earnest, the fight has ended or that, in a contest, an Ippon can be awarded. For Jodan techniques, the strikes should be without contact. For Chudan actions there should be a light contact. The attacker has to show that he could have seriously endangered the partner if he had not blocked properly. Direct counter-attacks (De-Ai) are not allowed in these cases.

In the counter-attack, a technique must be used that shows that the defender is able to achieve an Ippon. It is advisable not to counter-attack with the open hand or by executing a throw, because in this stage of training the mastering of Karate has not normally advanced sufficiently to come up to the criteria listed above.

Using a combination of techniques is usually a sign that the first counter-attack was inadequate. But, then this is exactly the aim of this exercise form, which is to show that you can use a perfect counter-attack to rapidly bring the fight to a conclusion.

5.2 JIYU - KUMITE

The name says it all: Now it's all about freestyle fighting. In contrast to all the other predetermined exercise Karate forms, and while still maintaining all the points from repertoire of techniques learned, the fighter's imagination is now called for. The basis for a Jiyu-Kumite is a solid training background in all areas of Karate. Success in fighting will not be possible without a sound knowledge of Kihon, the preparatory forms for free fighting (Kihon - Ippon Kumite and Jiyu - Ippon Kumite) and the Kata.

Which of the techniques can be used in free fighting depends on a number of factors. The fighter's temperament, his individual capability, his creativity, flexibility and, last not least, his physical condition are all factors that play a large role. Self-control is paramount. The attacks and counter-attacks may only be executed so that, at no time, will there be any danger to the safety of the partner or oneself.

The basis and criteria for this highest form of co-operative work with the partner – Jiyu Kumite – includes: a meaningful sense for fighting, a good feeling for the right distance to the partner, particularly well executed techniques, the ability to recognise and always gain an advantage, the ability to work towards an Ippon (contest point), physical strength and finally, fairness.

How can all this be brought together whilst moving about freely? Many Karateka are often overtaxed and frustrated in freestyle fighting, because they have already had bad experience with a lack of control and the resulting collection of bruises. The answer is simple – practice, practice, practice. There are, however, a few ground rules that are important.

Before you will be able to master the timing in order to achieve an Ippon with full Kime, you have to practice the particular specific Kumite style, so that you are quite at home with it and without having to exert a lot of energy. This exercise form of Randori must be practised intensely and, dependent on your ability to master the technique, at various paces. You use about 50% of your energy up in relaxed free fighting. The trainer should concentrate on the correct fighting posture, control, the right amount of snap back of the techniques as well as relaxed (but not slack) execution of defensive moves. As the training becomes routine, rapid, flowing dodging actions (Tai-Sabaki) and direct counter-attacks or rapidly executed open-handed defensive actions replace hard blocks, which have a good chance of causing bruising.

- Isolated training of individual situations in fighting with a partner can equally be of assistance. Here, the item to watch for is the exact end-point of the attack or counter-attack e.g., that the Mawashi-Geri ends at the Jodan region, also when executing this on the move, and not in front of the face or over the head, but exactly on the partner's chin or on his temple. Only when all the techniques in this form of training are correct, can one move on to improve flexibility and the feeling for different opponents and situations. Now one can start to get to grips with Kumite for contests with the aim of beating the opponent by achieving an Ippon or a Wazari.
- The best thing is to practice the techniques for a contest in all their different variations, such as: the attack, the direct counter-attack, the counter-attack after a block and combinations with preparatory actions.
- In free fighting as well as in the grading test, you should avoid techniques, which you cannot master yet, or which could be dangerous for the opponent. Empi, Nukite, dangerous throws or techniques aimed at the knee, soft parts of the body, larynx, eyes etc., have no place here.
- The elementary Kumite techniques Kizami-Zuki, Gyaku-Zuki, Uraken, Mawashi-Geri, Mae-Geri and Ashi-Barai as well as defence against them, including those with the open hand, have to be practised long and intensively before combinations are brought in. The early assimilation of these techniques in Kihon furthers the learning process. In Kumite – just as in self-defence (here also in combination with elbows and knees) – the valid maxims are that it must be executed with speed, simplicity and effectiveness. In each situation a reliable repertoire consisting of six or seven techniques is more use than the knowledge of artistic jumps and highly complicated Bunkai variations, which even in training can only function by virtue of the good will of the partner. Generally, the Karateka must be able to master the basic techniques of his style in any situation to perfection, in order to be able to use them as an effective weapon. It is the classic Kumite techniques that offer themselves as the most successful ones overall for this very good reason.
- In learning free fighting, it is important that you adapt to the typical Kumite sequence of movements. To do this, on the one hand, it's a question of practice, on the other hand, carefully watching successful fighting situations can help. You have

SHOTOKAN KARATE

to learn how you set up a technique, carry it out and in so doing, make use of the opportunity. The use of simply one technique is not sufficient in most cases, especially when you come up against Karateka in training, grading tests or contests, who have acquired a certain amount of knowledge. The work up to an attack using a feint or other technique is therefore enormously important in order to gain a successful action. The function of the feint is, for example, to mislead the opponent that you will go for the Jodan region, but you then attack the Chudan region. You can do this by faking a movement with your hips or by starting one technique but carrying out another. The situations with Kizami-Zuki, Gyaku-Zuki, Uraken, Mawashi-Geri, Mae-Geri, Ura-Mawashi-Geri and Ashi-Barai that follow, are examples of opportunities to achieve an Ippon.

An attack using Kizami-Zuki preceded by a feint

Using a Kizami-Zuki as a De-Ai counter-attack against an attack using Gyaku-Zuki. Kizami-Zuki used as a counter-attack against an attack with Mawashi-Geri

Kizami-Zuki in a combination with Gyaku-Zuki

Using a Gyaku-Zuki attack preceded by a feint

Gyaku-Zuki used as De-Ai against an attack with Mawashi-Geri

SHOTOKAN KARATE

A Gyaku-Zuki attack preceded by pushing down the arm

A Uraken attack preceded by a feint

A Mawashi-Geri attack preceded by a feint

A Mae-Geri attack preceded by a feint

A Ura-Mawashi-Geri attack preceded by a feint

An Ashi-Bari attack followed up with a Gyaku-Zuki.

SHOTOKAN KARATE

5.3   The Kata

5.3.1 Heian Shodan (First level)

Sequence of actions (unless otherwise stated all stances are in the Zenkutsu-Dachi position)

Starting position Hachi-Dachi (1)
Go left using Gedan-Barai (2)
Move forward with an Oi-Zuki (3)
Turn using a Gedan-Barai (4)
Bring the forward leg backwards delivering a Tettsui-Uchi (5)
Move forward delivering an Oi-Zuki (6)
Turn to the left using a Gedan-Barai (7)
Move forward with an Age-Uke on the right (8)
Move forward with an Age-Uke on the left (9)
Turn to the right using a Gedan-Barai and utter a Kiai (10)
Turn to the left using a Gedan-Barai (11)
Move forward with a left Oi-Zuki (12)
Turn to the right using a Gedan-Barai (13)
Move forward with a left Oi-Zuki (14)
Turn to the left using a Gedan-Barai (15)
Move forward with a right Oi-Zuki (16)
Move forward with a left Oi-Zuki (17)
Move forward with a right Oi-Zuki and utter a Kiai (18)
Turn to the left with a left Shuto-Uke into a Kokutsu-Dachi position (19)
Move forward turning 45º to the right with a Shuto-Uke into a Kokutsu-Dachi position (20)
Move back to the starting line with a right Shuto-Uke into a Kokutsu-Dachi position (21)
Move forward with a left Shuto-Uke into a Kokutsu-Dachi position (22)
Move back into the starting position (23)

HEIAN SHODAN

1

2

3

4

5

6

7

8

9

10

11

12

HEIAN SHODAN

13

14

15

16

17

18

19

20

21

22

23

5.3.2 Heian Nidan (Second level)

Sequence of actions:

From the starting position (1)
Go left leading in a Kokutsu-Dachi position and a double-block in Jodan (2)
Pull the left arm back to the shoulder and execute an Ura-Zuki with the right arm (3)
Counter-attack with a Zuki-Uke (4)
Bring the fist on to the left hip and move to the right into a Kokutsu-Dachi position with Jodan double-block (5)
Pull the right arm back to the shoulder and execute an Ura-Zuki with the left arm (6)
Counter-attack with a Zuki-Uke (7)
Swing back to execute a Yoko-Geri (8)
Execute a right-footed Yoko-Geri with Uraken (9)
Take up a Kokutsu-Dachi position and left Shoto-Uke (10)
Move forward in the Kokutsu-Dachi position with a right Shuto-Uke (11)
Move forward in the Kokutsu-Dachi position with a left Shuto-Uke (12)
Move forward in the Zenkutsu-Dachi position with a Nukite and utter a Kiai (13)
Turn in the Kokutsu-Dachi position with a left Shuto-Uke (14)
Move forward into a 45° Kokutsu-Dachi position with a right Shuto-Uke (15)
Transfer the left foot into a Zenkutsu-Dachi position and execute a right Gyaku-Uchi-Uke (16)
Execute a Mae-Geri with the right leg (19)
Place foot down and execute a right Gyaku-Zuki (23)
Move forward with a Morote-Uke in Zenkutsu-Dachi position (24)
Make a turn to the left with a left Gedan-Barai (25)
Move forward in a 45° angle making a right Age-Uke, uttering a Kiai (26)
Turn to the right with a Gedan-Barai (27)
Move forward in a 45° angle making a left Age-Uke, uttering a Kiai (28)
Return to the Hachi-Dachi position (29)

HEIAN NIDAN

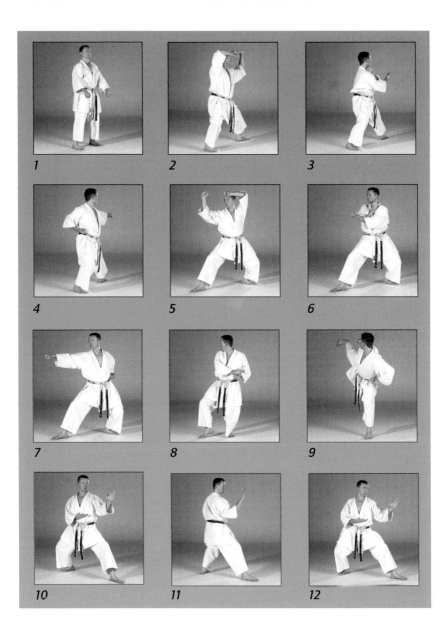

1

2

3

4

5

6

7

8

9

10

11

12

HEIAN NIDAN

13

14

15

16

17

18

19

20

21

HEIAN NIDAN

22

23

24

25

26

27

28

29

5.3.3 Heian Sandan (Third level)

From the starting position (1)
Go left leading in a Kokutsu-Dachi position with Uchi-Uke (2)
Stand up straight with a right Uchi-Uke and a left Gedan-Barai (3)
Standing upright, left Uchi-Uke and a right Gedan-Barai (4)
Leading with the right into a Kokutsu-Dachi position with a Uchi-Uke (5)
Standing upright, left Uchi-Uke and a right Gedan-Barai (6)
Standing upright, right Uchi-Uke and a left Gedan-Barai (7)
Move forward with a left Morote-Uke in Kokutsu-Dachi position (8)
Move forward in the Zenkutsu-Dachi position with a Nukite (9)
Twist round for a Tettsui-Uchi and do a left Tettsui-Uchi in the Kiba-Dachi position (10)
Move forward in the Zenkutsu-Dachi position with a right Oi-Zuki and utter a Kiai (11)
Pull the rear leg in and turn round, placing both fists on the hips (12)
Make a Fumikomi, leading with the right leg (13)
As the foot sets down, defend with the elbows (14)
and, use a right Tate-Uraken (15)
Make a Fumikomi, leading with the left leg (16)
As the foot sets down, defend with the elbows (17)
and, use a left Tate-Uraken (18)
Make a Fumikomi, leading with the right leg (19)
As the foot sets down, defend with the elbows (20)
and, use a right Tate-Uraken (21)
then, swing back with the right arm to execute a Tate-Shuto-Uke (22)
Move forward in the Zenkutsu-Dachi position with a left Oi-Zuki (23)
Bring the rear leg forward, then turn into a Kiba-Dachi position for a Mawashi-Zuki at the Jodan region and using a left Empi (24,25)
Glide back right into a Kiba-Dachi position and execute a left Mawashi-Zuki and right Empi uttering a Kiai (26)
Return to the Hachi-Dachi position (27)

HEIAN SANDAN

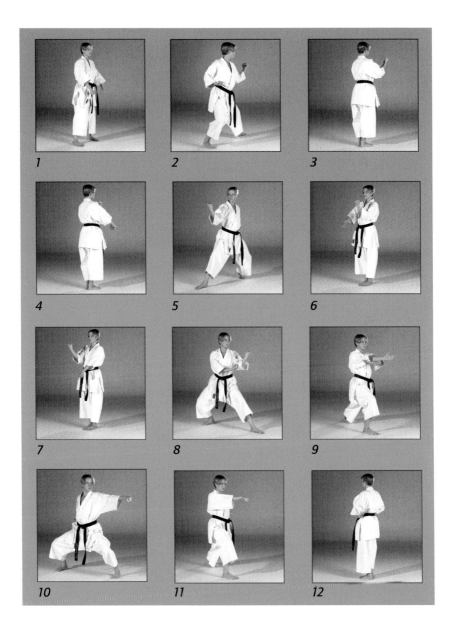

HEIAN SANDAN

13

14

15

16

17

18

19

20

21

22

23

24

HEIAN SANDAN

25

26

27

5.3.4 Heian Yondan (Fourth level)

Sequence of actions:

From the Hachi-Dachi starting position (1)
Pull the arm back with open hands (2)
Carry out an open-handed double-block into a left Kokutsu-Dachi position (3)
Go to the right (4)
with the same, slow movement (5)
Move forward in the Zenkutsu-Dachi position with a Gedan-Juji-Uke to the left (6)
Move forward with a Morote-Uke in Kokutsu-Dachi position (7)
Bring the fists on to the right hip (8)
and then execute a left-footed Yoko-Geri with Uraken (9)
When snapping back, the arm remains with the open hand (10)
Set down the foot and bring the Empi (elbow) forward (11)
Stand upright and with both fists on the left hip, swing back (12)
to execute a right-footed Yoko-Geri with Uraken (13)
When snapping back, the arm remains with the open hand (14)
And when setting down the foot, bring the Empi (elbow) forward (15)
From the Zenkutsu-Dachi position carry out a left arm Gedan-Shuto-Uke and simultaneously bring the right arm back (16)
Execute a right-handed Shuto-Uchi and defend left with an open-handed Age-Uke (17)
Execute a Mae-Geri (18)
Pull back and the place foot down with Uraken in Kosa-Dachi (19)
Here, you utter the first Kiai. Turn (20)
and come into a Kaki-Waki-Uke position in a Kokutsu-Dachi stance (21)
then execute a right-footed Mae-Geri (22)
and when setting down the foot do a right-armed Oi-Zuki (23)
and then a left-armed Gyaku-Zuki (24)
Right foot forward (25)
into a Kaki-Waki-Uke position in a Kokutsu-Dachi stance (26)
Move forward with left-footed Mae-Geri (27)

HEIAN YONDAN

and on setting down do a left-armed Oi-Zuki (28)
and then a right-armed Gyaku-Zuki (29)
Move forward in a left Kokutsu-Dachi position and Morote-Uke (30)
Move forward with a right Morote-Uke into the Kokutsu-Dachi position (31)
Move forward into a left Kokutsu-Dachi position and Morote-Uke (32)
Change over the left foot into Zenkutsu-Dachi position and stretch both arms out to the front with open hands (33)
Then execute a Hiza-Geri kick with the right knee and utter a Kiai (34)
Turn into a Kokutsu-Dachi position with a left-handed Shuto-Uke defence (35)
Move forward to the right with a Shuto-Uke into a Kokutsu-Dachi position (36)
Return to the Hachi-Dachi position (37)

HEIAN YONDAN

HEIAN YONDAN

HEIAN YONDAN

31 *32* *33*

34 *35* *36*

37

HEIAN GODAN

5.3.5 Heian Godan (Fifth level)

Sequence of actions:

Start in the Hachi-Dachi position (1)
Go to the left with a Uchi-Uke into the Kokutsu-Dachi position (2)
Staying in the same position do a Gyaku-Zuki (3)
Stand upright with a left-handed Kagi-Zuki (4)
Go to the right with a Uchi-Uke into the Kokutsu-Dachi position (5)
Staying in the same position do a Gyaku-Zuki (6)
Stand upright with a right-handed Kagi-Zuki (7)
Move forward with a right Morote-Uke into the Kokutsu-Dachi position (8)
Move forward with a Juji-Uke block into the Zenkutsu-Dachi position (9)
With open hands strike upwards for a Juji-Uke block in the Jodan region (10)
Close the hands and bring them back down onto the right-hand side of the body (11)
Defend using a left-handed Tate-Shuto-Uke (12)
Move forward with a right-handed Oi-Zuki in the Zenkutsu-Dachi position and utter a Kiai (13)
Carry out a Fumikomi into the other direction (14)
and as the foot is placed down do a Gedan-Barai with the right arm (15)
Pull the left arm back for a Heishu-Uke in the Chudan region (16)
Do a Mikazuki-Geri onto the left hand (17)
On setting the foot down into a Kiba-Dachi position use the Empi (18)
Pull the left leg up to the other one and carry out a right Morote-Uke into the Kosa-Dachi
position (19)
Stand up with a Morote-Ura-Zuki using the right arm while looking to the left (20)
Jump up (21)
and land with a Juji-Uke block in the Gedan region uttering a Kiai (22)
Go to the right with a Morote-Uke into the Zenkutsu-Dachi position (23)
Turn into the other direction with a right-handed Gedan-Nukite and a left-handed Nagashi-Uke (24)

HEIAN GODAN

Change into the Kenkutsu-Dachi position with a Gedan-Barai block and a Uchi-Uke in the Jodan region (25)
then bring the forward leg back into the Heisoku-Dachi position (26)
Turn and change arms. Do a Uchi-Uke in the Jodan region and a right-handed Gedan-Barai (27)
Move forward into the Zenkutsu-Dachi position and do a Nukite again, this time with the left hand. Block right with a Nagashi-Uke (28)
Change into the Kokutsu-Dachi position with a right-handed Gedan-Barai and a left-handed Uchi-Uke in Jodan region (29)
Return to the starting Hachi-Dachi position (30)

HEIAN GODAN

1

2

3

4

5

6

7

8

9

10

11

12

Kata

HEIAN GODAN

13

14

15

16

17

18

19

20

21

22

23

24

HEIAN GODAN

25

26

27

28

29

30

5.3.6 Tekki Shodan (Advanced first level)

Sequence of actions:

Start in the Hachi-Dachi position (1)

Place the feet together pulling in the right foot, place the right hand over the other (2)

Cross the right leg over the other (3)

Pulling back execute the start of a Fumikomi knee-lift (4)

Place the foot down and carry out a right-handed Haisho-Uke (5)

Remaining in the position grasp the Empi with the right hand (6)

Pull back both fists onto the right hip and look left (7)

Then block with a Gedan-Barai with the left arm (8)

Swing into a Kagi-Zuki with the right arm (9)

Transfer into a Kosa-Dachi position (10)

Pull back with the right arm and lift the left knee up (11)

Place the leg back down with a right-handed Uchi-Uke (12)

Carry out a right-handed Gedan-Uke and simultaneously defend with a Nagashi-Uke in the Jodan region (13)

Execute an Ura-Zuki with the left arm (14)

Look left and defend with a Nami-Ashi (15)

Place the leg down again and go to the right with a Morote-Uke (16)

Defend with a right-footed Nami-Ashi (17)

and go to the right with a Morote-Uke (18)

Pull back both fists onto the right hip (19)

Carry out a left-handed Chudan-Zuki and a Kagi-Zuki with the right arm ending with a Kiai (20)

Pull the left arm back and carry out a left-handed Haisho-Uke (21)

Grasp the Empi with the right hand (22)

Look right. Pull the fists back rapidly onto the left hip (23)

Carry out a right-handed Gedan-Uke (24)

Kagi-Zuki with the left arm (25)

Transfer into a Kosa-Dachi position (26)

Raise the right knee and pull back with the left arm (27)

Place the foot down again and defend with a left-arm Uchi-Uke (28)

Carry out a left-handed Gedan-Uke while at the same time pulling back for a Jodan-Nagashi-Uke (29)

TEKKI SHODAN

Deliver a right-handed Ura-Zuki (30)
Look right and then defend with a Nami-Ashi (31)
Place the foot down again with a Morote-Uke (32)
Execute a Nami-Ashi to the left (33)
and to the right with a Morote-Uke (34)
Pull back both fists onto the left hip (35)
and then carry out a right-handed Chudan-Zuki and a Kagi-Zuki with the left arm ending with a Kiai (36)
Place the left hand over the right hand (37)
Return to the starting Hachi-Dachi position (38)

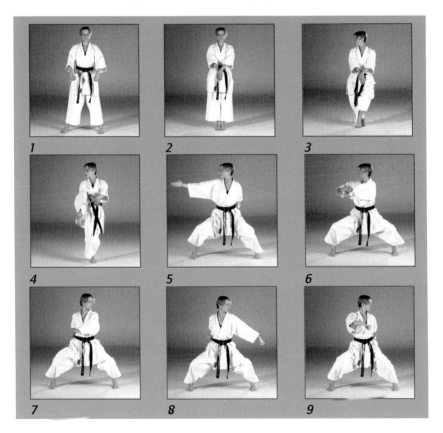

TEKKI SHODAN

TEKKI SHODAN

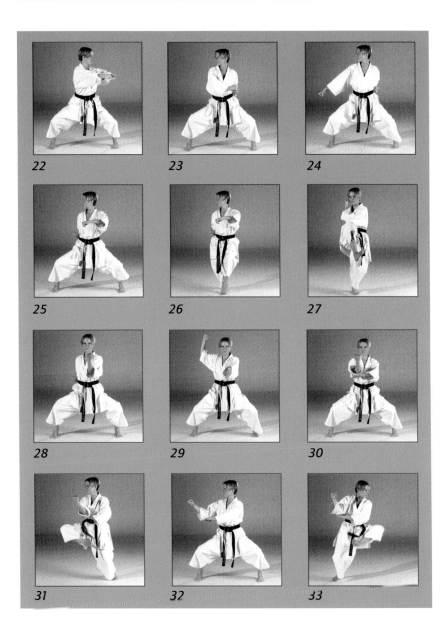

22

23

24

25

26

27

28

29

30

31

32

33

34   35   36

37   38

BASSAI-DAI

5.3.7 Bassai-Dai

The Bassai-Dai Kata is the most favoured Kata for the grading test for the 1st Dan. It is characterised by a very complex sequence of movements. With its rapid and dynamic movements from the hip area, and employing various defensive techniques, it requires intensive practice. The meaning of the words in its name "Bassai-Dai" is "to storm the fortress" and this describes its powerful character.

Sequence of actions:

Start in the Shizentai position (1)
Bring the feet together with the right coming alongside the left, while at the same time wrapping the left hand round the right clenched fist (2)
Make a spring-step forward leading with a rapid movement of the right knee (3)
Come up into a Kosa-Dachi position (4)
Turn round in the opposite direction into a Zenkutsu-Dachi position with a left-handed
Uchi-Uke (5)
Remaining in the same position carry out a right-handed Gyaku-Uchi-Uke (6)
Turn round in the opposite direction into a Zenkutsu-Dachi position with a left-handed
Gyaku-Soto-Uke (7)
Remaining in the same position carry out a right-handed Uchi-Uke (8)
Pull the left leg forward and do a scoop block in the Gedan region (9)
Move forward in the Zenkutsu-Dachi position with the right leg and block with a right-handed Soto-Uke (10,11)
Remaining in the same position carry out a left-handed Gyaku-Uchi-Uke (12)
Pull the left foot forward and pull back both fists onto the right hip. Adopt the Hachi-Dachi position (13)
Remaining in the same position, stretch out the left arm slowly into the Tate-Shuto-Uke defensive posture (14)
Execute a right-handed Choku-Zuki (15)
Turn the right hip forward carrying out a Uchi-Uke block (16)

Bring the hips forward parallel executing a right-handed Choku-Zuki (17)

Twist the hips carrying out a left-handed Uchi-Uke block (18)

Move forward into a right-footed Kokutsu-Dachi position with a Shuto-Uke (19)

Move forward into a left-footed Kokutsu-Dachi position with a Shuto-Uke (20)

Move forward into a right-footed Kokutsu-Dachi position with a Shuto-Uke (21)

Move back into a left-footed Kokutsu-Dachi position with a Shuto-Uke (22)

Change over into a Zenkutsu-Dachi position with a defensive Tsukami-Uke (23)

Execute a Yoko-Geri-Kekomi in the Gedan region uttering a Kiai (24,25)

Immediately turn into the Kenkutsu-Dachi position with a Shuto-Uke (26)

Move forward into a right-footed Kokutsu-Dachi position with a Shuto-Uke (27)

Bring the forward leg slowly backwards with a Morote-Uke in the Jodan region (28)

Execute a Hiza-Geri, ripping the arms apart (29)

Place the foot down firmly in a Fudo-Dachi manner executing a Hasami-Uchi (30)

Slip forward into the Zenkutsu-Dachi position with an Oi-Zuki strike (31)

Turn round executing a right-handed Gedan-Nukite (32)

Bring the forward leg slowly backwards with a right-handed Uchi-Uke in the Jodan region and a left-handed Gedan-Barai block (33)

Move forward with a Fumikomi knee-lift and a right handed Gedan-Barai in a Kiba-Dachi

position (34,35)

In the same position, pull back and go in the other direction carrying out a Haisho-Uke (36)

Carry out a right-footed Mikazuki-Geri, placing the foot down into the Kiba-Dachi position and executing a right-sided Mae-Empi (37,38)

Remaining in the same position defend with a right-handed Gedan-Uke (39)

Remaining in the same position defend with a left-handed Gedan-Uke (40)

Remaining in the same position defend with a right-handed Gedan-Uke (41)

Switch round to the right into a Zenkutsu-Dachi position executing a Yama-Zuki having brought the fists held for a short time from the left hip (42)

Bring back the forward leg and pull back the fists on to the right hip (43)

Go forward again in the Zenkutsu-Dachi position, executing a left-footed Hiza-Geri and a Yama-Zuki (on landing with the foot) and now with the left leg forward (44,45)

BASSAI-DAI

Pull the forward leg back and pull back both fists onto the left hip (46)

Go forward again executing a left-footed Hiza-Geri and a Yama-Zuki (on landing with the foot) into the Zenkutsu-Dachi position. Right leg forward (47,48)

Turn 90° right pulling back hard with the left arm in a large movement. Then defend downwards with a right-handed Sukui-Uke (49)

Carry out the same movement, this time right-handed (50)

Then pull the left leg to the right one and move forward into a Kokutsu-Dachi position with a Shuto-Uke executed at a 45° angle (51)

Move into a 90° angle without changing the technique - only the head and the eyes change direction (52,53)

Then pull the rear leg forward and move forward into a Kokutsu-Dachi position with a left-handed Shuto-Uke, uttering a Kiai (54,55)

Pull the forward leg back and return to the start position (56,57)

BASSAI-DAI

BASSAI-DAI

13

14

15

16

17

18

19

20

21

22

23

24

BASSAI-DAI

BASSAI-DAI

37

38

39

40

41

42

43

44

45

46

47

48

BASSAI-DAI

49

50

51

52

53

54

55

56

57

BIBLIOGRAPHY

6.1 Bibliography

ENOEDA, K.: Shotokan Karate Advanced Kata Vol. 1-3. Norwich 1983.

ENOEDA, K.: Shotokan Karate 10th Kyu to 6th Kyu. London 1996.

ENOEDA, K.: Shotokan Karate 5th Kyu to Black Belt. London 1996.

EVANS. B./CHRISTOPHER, R.: Get to Grips with Competition Karate. London 1997.

FUNAKOSHI, G.: Karate-do Kyohan.Tokio 1978.

FUNAKOSHI, G.: Karate-do: Mein Weg. Weidental 1983.

GURSHARAN, S.: The Advanced Shotokan Karate Handbook. Bedford 1997.

HASSELL, R. G.: Gespräche mit dem Meister Masatoshi Nakayama. Lauda 1999.

HASSELL, R. G.: Shotokan Karate: Its History and Evolution. St. Louis 1998.

HILLEBRECHT/HILLEBRECHT:
Übungsprogramme zur Dehn- und Kräftigungsgymnastik. Aachen 1998.

JAKHEL, R.: Modern Sports Karate. Aachen 2000.

KANAZAWA, H.: Shotokan Kata Band 1-2. Tokio 1982.

KANAZAWA, H.: Kumite Kyohan. Tokio 1987.

KARAMITSOS, E./PEJCIC,B.: Karate Grundlagen. Niedernhausen 1997.

KNEBEL, K. P.: Funktionsgymnastik. Hamburg 1985.

MILON, M.: Apprenez vos Katas de Base du Karaté Shotokan. Paris 1997.

NAKAYAMA, M.: Karate-Do. Dynamic Karate. Sprendlingen 1972.

NAKAYAMA, M.: Nakayamas Karate perfekt. Band 1-8. Niedernhausen 1989.

NAKAYAMA, M.: Best Karate. Band 9-11. Tokio, New York, London, 1989.

NAKAYAMA, M.: Karate zur Selbstverteidigung 1. Niedernhausen 1994.

NAKAYAMA, M.: Karate zur Selbstverteidigung 2. Niedernhausen 1994.

OKAZAKI,T./STRICEVIC, M.V.: Modernes Karate. Niedernhausen 1994.

REILLY, R. L.: Complete Shotokan Karate. Boston 1998.

SCHLATT: Shotokan No Hyakkajiten. Lauda 1995.

TANAKA, M.: Kumite in Perfektion. Lauda 1997.

WICHMANN, W. D.: Richtig Karate. München 1994.

WICHMANN, W. D.: Richtig Selbstverteidigen. München 1990.

WICHMANN, W. D.: Kata 1-3. Niedernhausen 1985, 1986, 1990.

6.2 Glossary

Japanese Technical Terms

A

Age-Uke	A rising defensive block
Antei	Balance, equilibrium
Ashi-Barai	Leg sweep attack
Atemi-points	Vital points on the body
Awasete	...equals...

B

Barai	Sweeping movement
Bunkai	Demonstrating techniques of a Kata with a partner
Budo	Japanese martial arts in general

C

Choku-Zuki	A straight punch from the Hachi-Dachi
Chudan	Mid-section of the body chest height

D

Dachi	Stance / position
Dai	Big, great
Dan	Black belt grade, grade of master
De-Ai	A counter-attack while at the same time defending successfully
Do	The path to spiritual and good moral behaviour
Dojo	The training hall

E

Embusen	Diagram of the steps for a Kata
Empi	Elbow
Empi-Uchi	An attack delivered with the elbow

GLOSSARY

F

Fudo	Firm, deeply rooted
Fumi	Stamping movement with the foot
Fumikomi-Achi	A step made with a stamping movement

G

Gaiwan	Outer edge of the arm
Gedan	Lower area of the body, below the belt area
Gedan-Barai	Blocking an attack with a downwards movement
Gohon-Kumite	Five-step prearranged sparring
Gyaku	Reverse side to the forward leg
Gyaku-Zuki	Reverse punch (e.g., left foot forward, right Zuki)

H

Haisho-Uke	Backhand block
Haito	The (sword) edge of the hand
Haiwan	The upper edge of the arm
Hajime	"Begin!" The command given for opponents to start a contest
Hangetsu-Dachi	'Half-moon' or crescent posture
Hanmi	Stance with the hips half-turned to one side
Hara	'Belly', centre of the body, the body's spiritual and inner centre of gravity
Hasami-Uchi	Strike with a scissor action
Heisoku-Dachi	Standing posture, feet joined together
Heishu	'Adams apple'
Hidari	Left
Hikite	Series of movements conducted as a technique as the arm is pulled backwards
Hiza	Knee

I

Ippon	A full point
Ippon-Kumite	An attack using only one technique (step)

GLOSSARY

J

Jogai	Outside the limits of the mat contest area
Jiyu	Freestyle
Jiyu-Kumite	Freestyle fighting
Jiyu-Ippon-Kumite	Freestyle one-step sparring
Jodan	Upper level (Head and neck height)
Juji-Uke	Cross hands/wrists block

K

Kachi	Contest winner
Kaeshi-Ippon-Kumite	Sequence with reverse one-step attack
Kagi-Zuki	A swinging hooked punch
Kai-Ashi	step
Kakato	Heel
Kaki-Wake-Uke	Block using crossed arms
Kamae	Starting position, guard
Karateka	Anyone who practises Karate
Karate-Gi	Karate training uniform/dress
Kata	Form, sequence
Keage	Kick with a withdrawing whipping action
Kekomi	A penetrating kick
Keri	Kick (also spelled Geri)
Kiai	Karate shout
Kiba-Dachi	Sideways posture, legs apart
Kihon	A basic movement/technique
Kime	Focussing all one's physical and psychological force (at the end of the technique)
Kizami-Zuki	A punch with the forward arm
Kokutsu-Dachi	Upright stance leaning back on the rear leg
Kumite	Sparring with a partner

M

Mae	Front, in front
Mae-Ashi-Geri	A front kick with the leading leg
Mae-Empi	front attack with the elbow held level
Mae-Geri	A kick to the front with the rear leg

GLOSSARY

Makiwara	Woven raffia tied to a post for punch training
Mawashi-Geri	A roundhouse kick (mawashi - 'in a circle')
Mawate	Turn
Migi	Right, on the right, right hand side
Mikazuki-Geri	A crescent kick describing an arc of a circle
Mokuso	A meditative posture for concentrating and breathing with closed eyes
Morote-Uchi-Ude-Uke	Defence of the middle area using locked hands from the inside
Musubi-Dachi	Feet positioned at 60° apart, heels touching together

N

Nagashi-Uke	Defence block using the inside of the forearm
Naiwan	Inside of the arm
Nami-Ashi	Blocking movement by bending the leg up to protect the target
Neko-Ashi-Dachi	'Cat stance', the weight of the body is almost completely over the rear leg
Nukite	Stabbing blow (the hand is held vertically to the ground)

O

Oi-Zuki	Straight fist punch/lunge punch
Otagani-Rei	Formal bow of greeting to the other training participants
Otoshi-Uke	Defence from above downwards

R

Randori	Free-fighting
Rei	Karate bow, greeting
Ren-Geri	Two-step kicking movement
Ren-Zuki	Alternate punches

S

Sabaki	Dodging movement (also Tai-Sabaki)
Sanbon-Kumite	Three-step sparring
Sanbon-Zuki	Alternate punches in threes

GLOSSARY

Sanchin-Dachi	Standing stance with knees and feet turned in to protect the lower abdomen
Seiza	Kneeling posture sitting on the heels at the beginning and end of training
Sensei-Ni-Rei	Formal bow of greeting to training teacher
Shiai	Competition
Shitei Kata	Compulsory Kata
Shizentai	Natural basic posture with the feet shoulder width apart
Shomen	Centred to the front
Shuto-Uchi	Direct attack with the 'sword-hand', edge of the hand
Shuto-Uke	Defensive movement edge of the hand
Shuwan	Underside of the arm
Sochin-Dachi	Position in the Kata Sochin (alternative name is Fudo-Dachi)
Soto-Uke	Defensive block using the outer edge of the forearm from the inside to the outside
Suri-Ashi	Sliding step (starting with the front foot)
Sukui-Uke	Spoon block using one arm
T	
Tate-Empi	A rising elbow blow
Tate-Shuto-Uke	Blocking a blow using the edge of the hand stretched out
Tate-Uraken-Uchi	Defence using the back of the hand held vertically
Tate-Zuki	A punch delivered with the fist, palm along a vertical plane
Te	Hand
Teisho	Base of the palm of the hand
Teisho-Uke	Block with palm of the hand
Te-Otoshi-Uke	Hand block from above downwards - the palm of the hand is parallel to the ground
Tettsui-Uchi	Fist blow using the back (little finger) edge of the hand in a reaping action
Tokui Kata	'Favourite' kata

GLOSSARY

Tori	The attacker
Tsugi-Ashi	Sliding the feet forward one after the other - rear foot first
Tsukami-Uke	Blocking a blow by seizing opponent's arm or leg
Tsuki	Blow, punch (also spelled Zuki)

U

Uchi	Strike
Uchi-Ude-Uke	Inside arm block of the middle zone
Ude	Forearm
Uke	A defensive movement
Uraken-Uchi	Strike with the back of the fist
Ura-Mawashi-Geri	Roundhouse with the heel or sole of the foot
Ura-Zuki	Blow with the fist held close to the body
Ushiro-Geri	A back kick

W

Waza	Technique
Wazari	A half-point

Y

Yama-Zuki	"Mountain fist". A wide U-shaped double punch using both hands
Yame	Stop!
Yoi	"Get ready!" (This command is used to signal the adoption of the Shizentai starting posture
Yoko	Lateral, side
Yoko-Geri	Side-kick
Yoko-Uraken-Uchi	Sideways strike with the back of the hand
Yori-Ashi	Sideways sliding movement

Z

Zanshin	Vigilance, constant concentration
Zenkutsu-Dachi	Position with weight on forward leg
Zuki	Blow, punch (also spelled Tsuki)

Appendix

ACKNOWLEDGEMENTS

Acknowledgements

I would like to express my thanks and gratitude to all those, without whose assistance this book would not have been possible: Tanja Schwabe, Lorin Wehr, Angelo Martin, John Dahl and Torsten Neuhof for their patience as performers for the photography. Benedikt Sommer and Tanja Schwabe for their suggestions regarding the contents as well as Christian and Roland Fritsch from Fotostudio FTB-Werbefotografie Berlin for their professionalism and patience, and Gerhard Axmann for the cover design.

PHOTO & ILLUSTRATION CREDITS

Photo & Illustration Credits

Cover Photo, Photos: Christian and Roland Fritsch, Fotostudio
FTB - Werbefotografie, Berlin

Cover Design: Birgit Engelen

More Karate

Rudolf Jakhel
Modern Sports Karate
Basics of Techniques & Tactics

In this book the author analyses karate techniques commonly preferred by contestants in sport bouts. Written in an understandable language, the book profoundly explains the kinetic composition of the individual fighting actions and their mutual relationships, as well as systematically revealing the core ingredients of tactics in combat. With its detailed descriptions and approximately 340 photos, drawings, diagrams and tables, the book will appeal to karate sportsmen and women of all karate styles.

2nd edition
168 pages, 320 photos
321 figures, 5 tables
Paperback, 14.8 x 21 cm
ISBN 1-84126-042-8
£ 12.95 UK/
$ 17.95 US/$ 25.95 CDN

MEYER &MEYER SPORT

If you are interested in
Meyer & Meyer Sport
and our large
programme, please
visit us **online**
or call our **Hotline** ▼

online:
▶ **www.meyer-meyer-sports.com**

▶ **Hotline**:
+49 (0)1 80 / 5 10 11 15

We are looking
forward to your call!

Please order our catalogue!
Please order our catalogue!

MEYER &MEYER SPORT

MEYER & MEYER Verlag | Von-Coels-Straße 390 | D-52080 Aachen, Germany | Fax +49 (0)2 41 - 9 58 10-10

Z10F/Anz 10/01